D1533251

HEARST MARINE BOOKS
COMPLETE GUIDE
TO ANCHORING AND
LINE HANDLING

HEARST MARINE BOOKS COMPLETE GUIDE TO ANCHORING AND LINE HANDLING

PUTTING ROPE TO WORK FOR YOU

David G. Brown

Photographs by Carol B. Brown
Illustrations by Christine Erikson

HEARST MARINE BOOKS
New York

Copyright © 1996 by David G. Brown

All rights reserved. No part of this book may be reproduced or utilized in any form or by any means, electronic or mechanical, including photocopying, recording, or by any information storage or retrieval system, without permission in writing from the Publisher. Inquiries should be addressed to Permissions Department, William Morrow and Company, Inc., 1350 Avenue of the Americas, New York, N.Y. 10019.

It is the policy of William Morrow and Company, Inc., and its imprints and affiliates, recognizing the importance of preserving what has been written, to print the books we publish on acid-free paper, and we exert our best efforts to that end.

Library of Congress Cataloging-in-Publication Data

Brown, David G. (David Geren), 1944-
    Hearst Marine Books complete guide to anchoring and line handling:
    putting rope to work for you / David G. Brown; with photos by
    Carol B. Brown.
    Includes index.
    ISBN 0-688-13734-2
    1. Anchorage. 2. Marline spike seamanship. 3. Rope. I. Title
VM791.B76 1996
623.88'82—dc20   95-15925
                                                                      CIP

Printed in the United States of America

First Edition

1 2 3 4 5 6 7 8 9 10

Produced for Hearst Books by
Michael Mouland & Associates,
Toronto

Book design by Mimi Maxwell

This book is dedicated to the Cleveland, Ohio, sailors who serve as volunteer crew aboard Edgewater Yacht Club's race committee boat, *The Ark*. Their unselfish work manhandling the anchor has allowed me to gather enormous amounts of firsthand knowledge about anchors and anchoring without fatiguing myself. Thanks, guys!

PREFACE

This is not another marlinespike book about tying obscure knots or fashioning decorative coach whipping. There are more than enough of those already. Instead, this book focuses on applying modern rope, equipment, and techniques to having more fun boating. Personal free time is scarce these days. Most of us would rather be on the water than learning the complexities of splicing or knotting a running Turk's head. We save precious time by purchasing prespliced dock lines cut to working length. Time once spent splicing is thus saved for gunkholing, racing around the buoys, or just enjoying a cool one in the cockpit at sunset.

Of course, knowledge of a few basic knots is necessary. But these are simple and easily mastered. Anyone can learn to tie a cleat hitch, or a bowline, or throw a round turn and two half hitches. Sailors may want to add a square knot, a rolling hitch, or a stopper knot to their repertoires. Beyond that, there's little need in modern boating to learn the more obscure knots—that is, unless you decide to make marlinespike seamanship into a hobby of its own. (There are actually knot-tying clubs!)

No other equipment on a modern pleasure boat shares the antiquity of anchors and rope. Both have been aboard vessels from the very earliest days of seafaring. Long before the dawn of the Christian era, the ship's anchor served as a symbol of hope and security. Perhaps the antiquity of rope and anchors explains why so much of what is in print does not apply to modern boating. Technology changes quickly, but traditions do not.

An illustration of that change is the actual stuff rope is made of. It makes little sense to discuss the care of natural-fiber rope these days. Synthetic fibers have supplanted manila, hemp, and sisal on cordage aboard U.S. pleasure boats. So this book focuses on modern synthetics at the expense of natural fibers. The intention isn't to flout tradition, but to keep the focus on information of direct benefit to the reader.

ACKNOWLEDGMENTS

Many thanks to everyone at the West Marine store in Port Clinton, Ohio, for helping with many of the photographs in this book.

CONTENTS

1

MODERN SYNTHETIC ROPE

"Knowing the ropes" is the traditional measure of seamanship. And this knowledge is just as important today as it was a century ago aboard sailing ships. The only difference is that the materials have changed. Just as fiberglass replaced wood for boats, synthetics have supplanted natural fibers for rope. Natural manila, sisal, and hemp fibers have disappeared from the modern marine store. Taking their place are synthetic fibers such as nylon, Dacron, and polypropylene. These factory-made fibers are stronger and longer-lasting than any of the natural materials they replaced. "Knowing the ropes" today requires a smattering of chemistry and a dash of engineering in addition to old-fashioned seamanship.

Synthetic fibers are made of individual filaments (or strands) that are "engineered" to have special properties not found in nature. For instance, nylon rope is engineered with plenty of spring to absorb shock loads common in mooring and anchoring. And Dacron rope is specially treated to resist stretching under load, making it ideal for sailboat halyards. The physical characteristics of synthetic fibers are further enhanced by the mechanical construction of the rope. The manner in which fibers are twisted or woven influences both the rope's stretch and its breaking strength.

Color is another aspect of modern synthetic ropes. Manila or sisal display only their natural dull buff color. Synthetic fibers allow every rope on the boat to be a different, bold hue. Color-coded ropes aboard racing sailboats prevent mistakes. A blue genoa sheet isn't likely to be confused with a red spinnaker guy. One manufacturer even produces rope that glows in the dark! This glow-in-the-dark rope is sold as a safety device for night rescues or as a visible warning of danger. Its inventor saw the need after tripping over a tent rope on a Boy Scout camping trip with his son.

Rope remains a very simple product despite the complexities of fiber, construction, and color. Three-strand laid (twisted) construction popular for anchor and dock lines traces its roots back to ancient Egypt and beyond. Papyrus ropes made for the pharaohs' ships in ancient Egypt were little different in construction from today's three-strand nylon rope.

Modern woven "yacht braid" ropes trace their roots to the Industrial Revolution and the development of complex weaving machines. Over a century ago, sailors on clipper ships knew braided ropes as *sennits*. The quaint old name has dropped from use, but braided rope is growing in popularity.

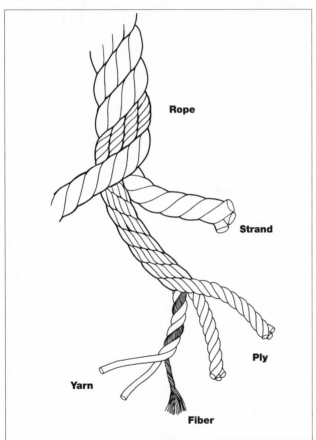

High-quality twisted rope is made using a four-phase construction. Individual fibers are twisted into yarns, then plies, which are twisted into strands. Final twisting of the strands produces the rope. The direction of twist is reversed with each phase.

ROPE CONSTRUCTION

Three-Strand Laid Rope

The most common form of rope is the conventional three-strand twisted variety. Synthetic rope available in marine stores today is right-hand laid: the final twists of the three strands are made to the right (clockwise). There was a time when four- and five-strand ropes were common and all could be had in left-hand lay as well. Such exotic rope products are available these days only on special order—if they're available at all.

Friction and twisting are the forces that hold a three-strand rope together and provide much of its strength. The best ropes are made in a four-step (or four-phase) process that starts by twisting individual fibers into yarns, which in turn are twisted into plies. The plies are then twisted into strands. The final twisting marries three strands into a finished rope. Each of these twistings is done in the opposite direction to the previous step: yarns are twisted left, plies right, strands left, and the final rope right.

Reversing twists at each stage of construction helps the rope stay together rather than unravel. If the plies try to untwist, they can do it only by twisting the strands tighter together. The amount of twist imparted at each stage determines whether a rope is said to be *hard lay* or *soft lay.* Surprisingly, hard-lay rope has slightly more stretch than a soft-lay line. It also tends to be more round in cross-section, making it behave better when rove through blocks or fairleads.

More important than the hardness of the lay is the evenness of the twisting. In theory, every strand, ply, yarn, and filament should take an equal share of the load. Well-made ropes come very close to this theoretical perfection, particularly in the load sharing of the three main strands. Less-well-made ropes tend to load one strand more than the other two. Uneven loading causes the line to untwist under strain. This rotation often causes unexpected difficulties. A poorly made rope seems to untie knots or pull the anchor out of the bottom.

Small-diameter and less-expensive ropes are made using a three-step process that eliminates the step of twisting yarns into plies. With nylon, the difference between four- and three-step ropes can be significant. As any woman who has worn hosiery knows, individual nylon filaments are subject to snagging. Three-step rope exposes these filaments along more of their length than does four-step construction. As a result, three-stage rope is more likely to suffer snags and chafe.

Physical Characteristics of Good Three-Strand Rope

• Four-stage (four-phase) construction consisting of filaments, yarns, plies, and strands.
• Smooth, even twisting throughout construction, but particularly in the final twisting of strands into rope. As a rule, the better ropes have more

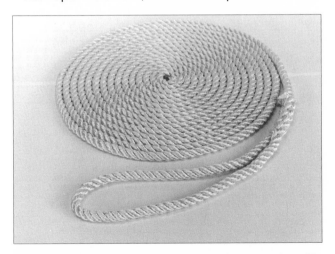

Well-made twisted rope has a smooth, round cross-section with even twisting throughout. It handles easily with little tendency to hockle. *(Courtesy Rope Works)*

twists in a given length than low-quality rope.
• The cross-section of high-quality rope appears nearly round rather than with three pronounced lobes.

Manufacturers use a variety of processes to "finish" rope after the final twisting. Heat and moisture in combination change nylon so that it does not shrink when exposed to the weather. Chemical lubricants impregnated into the filaments reduce internal friction and increase chafe resistance.

Braided Rope Construction

There are dozens of ways to construct braided rope. In the United States, the two most popular are *double braid* (also called yacht braid or braid-on-braid) and *plaited* (or four-strand sennit). Double-braid ropes are commonly used for sailboat rigging and dock lines. Other types of construction seen infrequently include hollow braid, which has no core, and stuffer-braid rope, which has a yarn core. Solid-braid rope is relatively hard and stiff, but the ⅛-inch-diameter size can be used for flag halyards.

Double-braid rope is technically two square sennits, one woven around the other. Although expensive, this construction results in a rope that is about 20 percent stronger than an equal diameter three-strand laid rope. The nature of this construction makes the core and the outer braids share the load equally. But only the outer braid is subject to chafe and snagging. Anyone willing to buy the special tools and take the time to learn the procedure can splice double-braid rope.

Plaited polypropylene is often used for dinghy painters and ski tow lines. Plaited construction involves weaving (plaiting) of eight plies into a four-strand sennit. Four of the strands have a right twist and four a left twist. An advantage of this type of construction is that it can be spliced as easily as three-strand twisted lay rope.

Comparison: Twist Versus Braid

As the old sailor's saying goes, "Different ropes for different ships." Neither twist nor braid rope does all jobs equally well. In choosing the proper rope there are several considerations:

Table 1-1
Rope Comparison Table

TWISTED LAY ROPE	BRAIDED ROPE
• Lower initial cost and better availability	• Stronger, less stretch in equal sizes to twist
• Easiest to splice	• Holds knots better
• Allows variety of knots and bends	• Runs through blocks and fairleads better
• Greater stretch	• Higher initial cost and less availability
• Harder on the hands	

Double-braid construction is considered superior to three-strand twisted lay rope in nearly all applications, but *only* when cost is not considered. It's preferred for sailboat run-

Table 1-2
Typical Uses

USE	THREE-STRAND TWISTED	DOUBLE BRAID
Anchor Line	Excellent (Low Cost)	Very Good (Expensive)
Dock Lines (Permanent)	Very Good	Excellent
Dock Lines (Transient)	Excellent (Expensive)	Very Good
Halyards	Good	Excellent
Sail Sheets	Fair	Excellent

ning rigging because it works well on winches and is easier on the hands. Other than higher cost, complicated splicing is the significant disadvantage of braided rope. People who make up their own mooring and anchor lines often choose twisted lay rope because it is easier to splice. The lower cost of twisted rope makes it popular for long anchor lines where the money saved can be substantial.

Table 1-3
Typical Rope Breaking Strengths (in pounds)

NOMINAL DIAMETER	3-STRAND TWISTED NYLON	DOUBLE-BRAIDED DACRON	3-STRAND TWISTED POLYPROPYLENE	TWISTED MANILA
1/4"	2,000	2,500	1,350	600
3/8"	4,400	4,900	2,900	1,350
1/2"	7,500	8,500	4,700	2,650
5/8"	12,200	14,600	6,000	4,400
3/4"	16,700	18,400	7,900	5,400
1"	29,400	31,000	3,000	9,000

GENERAL ROPE CHARACTERISTICS

Breaking Strength

No matter which fiber or what the construction, all ropes have an ultimate breaking strength. This is sometimes called the *tensile strength*, although most rope manufacturers use the simpler term. *Breaking strength* refers to the ultimate strain that a rope can endure before coming apart. In the United States, breaking strengths are given in terms of pounds.

Breaking strength is determined by scientific testing under controlled conditions in a laboratory. A length of rope is stretched by a hydraulic cylinder until the fibers fail. The force needed to break the rope is recorded by sophisticated electronic instruments, which also indicate other characteristics such as stretch and elastic limits. Rope breaking strength varies from brand to brand. Spun or short-staple yarns have lower breaking strengths than continuous-filament yarns. Ratings given in Table 1-3 should be considered as guidelines only. Consult the rope manufacturer for specific breaking strength and safe working load data on the rope under consideration.

Safe Working Load

Breaking strength is an interesting number, but more important is the *safe working load*, which is the maximum weight the rope can support in repeated loadings without damage. It is always a fraction of the rope's ultimate breaking strength. Dividing the breaking strength by the safe working load gives the rope's safety factor:

$$\text{Safety factor} = \frac{\text{Breaking strength}}{\text{Safe working load}}$$

Safety factor is normally expressed as a ratio. If the breaking strength of a rope is 4,000 pounds and the safe working load is rated at 1,000 pounds, the safety factor is said to be "four to one," or 4:1. In this example, the safe working load is 25 percent of the breaking strength.

$$\frac{4,000}{1,000} = 4$$

1,000 = 25% of 4,000

Appropriate working loads for all types of rope are set at specified percentages of maximum breaking strength to provide an acceptable safety factor. The American Boat and Yacht Council (ABYC) recommends working loads at the following percentages of breaking strength:

Three-Strand Twisted Nylon **11%**
Double-Braided Dacron **20%**
Polypropylene **17%**

Table 1-4 shows typical working loads for ropes of various diameters. This table should be considered as a guideline only. Consult the manufacturer of your rope for specific ratings.

Table 1-4

Typical Working Loads (in pounds)			
NOMINAL DIAMETER	3-STRAND TWISTED NYLON	DOUBLE-BRAIDED DACRON	3-STRAND TWISTED POLYPROPYLENE
1/4"	182	420	213
3/8"	407	750	459
1/2"	704	1,400	714
5/8"	1,144	2,400	1,054
3/4"	1,562	3,000	1,445
1"	2,750	5,600	2,380

Stretch

Within limits, all fibers (natural or synthetic) are elastic, and each has its unique limit of elasticity. As long as that limit is not exceeded, any fiber will stretch under load and then return to its original length when the load is released. Add too much load, however, and the fiber stretches beyond its limit of elasticity. This damages the structure of the fiber so it cannot return to its original length. A rope that has been stretched beyond its elastic limit is always weaker than one that has not.

Nylon is the champion when it comes to stretch. Depending upon construction, a nylon rope may stretch up to 40 percent of its original length. Dacron, another synthetic, stretches only 10 percent of its original length, and that stretch factor is often reduced further in the manufacturing process. Polypropylene, the third most popular synthetic for pleasure boat rope, has virtually no stretch.

Construction of the rope (twist, braid, or plait) also plays a part in a rope's ability to stretch under load. A three-strand rope tends to stretch more under load than a braided rope. Each strand untwists slightly, which produces a small amount of extra length. Knowing the stretch characteristic of both the fiber and the construction is critical to choosing the correct rope for a given task.

Chafe Resistance

Chafe is the wearing away of the individual fibers of a rope. It is caused by friction as the rope is pulled over a rough edge or sharp-radius bend. The ability to resist chafe is critical in mooring lines, which must do their job for long periods of time unattended. Some synthetic fibers are naturally resistant to chafe while others have little or no resistance. High-quality ropes have chemicals impregnated in the filaments to increase chafe resistance.

SYNTHETIC FILAMENTS

Rope has been made out of virtually every fiber, natural or synthetic, that can be twisted or woven. If it were not for rot, natural-fiber rope would still be strong competition against more expensive synthetics. Natural fibers are strong and usually cost far less than their man-made cousins. But they are all subject to rapid deterioration through various processes lumped together as "rot." Limited service life means that natural fibers aren't as cost-effective as the more expensive, but longer-lived, synthetic fibers.

A wide variety of synthetic fibers are now on the market. Many are just brand names for common generic fibers such as nylon or Dacron. Of the available synthetics, only a relative handful are used for marine rope:

> ### Nylon
>
> **Strength: Very high**
> **Stretch: High**
> **Construction: Three-strand twist or double braid**
> **Primary Uses: Dock lines, anchor lines**
> **Cost: Moderate**

Nylon was the first synthetic yarn. Wallace H. Carothers began working on this polymer for E. I. du Pont de Nemours & Company in the late 1920s. By 1938, the company had a pilot plant in Wilmington, Delaware, producing his synthetic fiber. The word *nylon* became firmly associated with women's hosiery by the 1940s, an association it still retains. Nylon rope made its appearance during the late 1950s on pleasure boats, where it quickly supplanted manila and other natural fibers.

The term *nylon* is a generic covering a wide family of filaments with similar chemistry. These filaments are sold under a variety of trade names: Caprolan, Perlon, Antron, Cadron, etc. Some variations are created by changing the cross-section of the filament from round to triangular or cruciform. Other variations differ in the molecular structure of the filament. The majority made in the United States is of the *nylon 66* variety, while production of *nylon 6* is common in Europe.

Manufacture of nylon filament for rope starts by melting nylon chips under a nitrogen atmosphere to prevent contamination from air pollution. Molten nylon is extruded through extremely fine orifices at a temperature of nearly 300 degrees F. These orifices may be circular or various geometric shapes, depending upon the final use of the filament. At this point, extruded nylon has a rather dull appearance and does not yet have its full strength. The glossy sheen associated with nylon comes from cold drawing through pressure rollers during a later processing step.

Nylon stretches from 11 to 15 percent of its original length without damage. Laboratory tests show that filaments stretched 16 percent have a 91 percent recovery of their original lengths. Stretching beyond this point permanently damages the filament, but breakage does not occur until elongation reaches approximately 22 percent. This high elasticity of raw nylon filament is retained during the twisting or weaving of rope.

Nylon has a specific gravity of 1.14, which makes it slightly heavier than water. It will not float, but sinks very slowly. Wet nylon absorbs 10 to 15 percent of its dry weight while retaining up to 90 percent of its dry strength. Nylon also suffers little loss in strength from exposure to mild acids or alkalies.

A low melting point is nylon's major drawback. It becomes sticky at 170 degrees C and melts in air at a temperature of about 250 degrees C. Temperatures above 230 degrees C will damage nylon filaments. While not fireproof, nylon does not burn well and the fibers in rope will not sustain combustion. Nylon melts to a glassy globule, giving rise to the use of heat to seal the ends of rope to keep it from unraveling.

Nylon's ability to elongate under load makes it ideal for dock lines and anchoring where stretch helps snub shock loads. Stretch can be an advantage when towing another boat, but it also has drawbacks. Heavily loaded nylon rope exhibits the "slingshot effect" if a cleat pulls off one of the boats. Because nylon does not absorb significant amounts of water, it does not become heavier when used as an anchor rode. Nylon rope does not rot, but must be protected from chafe. Breakage usually occurs near splices.

Dacron

Strength: Very high
Stretch: Low
Construction: Double braid, some three-strand twist
Primary Use: Sailboat running rigging
Cost: High

This linear polymeric fiber was developed in England by chemists working for the Calico Printers Association. It is a direct outgrowth of nylon in the United States. In England this fiber is called Terylene, while it's known as Dacron in North America. Both names refer to the same filament and do not reflect any substantial differences.

Raw material for Dacron is crude oil processed into ethylene glycol. This is combined with terephthalic acid at high temperatures in a vacuum. The resulting polymer is extruded as a ribbon, which is cut into chips. Later, these chips are melted and filaments extruded in a process similar to that for nylon. In the final step, the filaments are drawn to about five times their original length. The amount of drawing determines the stretch characteristics of the final yarn. Extremely low-stretch yarns for rope are drawn out more than yarns for other uses.

In many respects, Dacron resembles nylon. Both are strong either wet or dry. Unlike nylon, however, Dacron is affected by alkalies, especially at higher temperatures. Depending upon the drawing process, Dacron can be produced in a range of stretch characteristics. Filaments intended for marine rope are manufactured to stretch less than

3 percent when loaded to 15 percent of their breaking strengths.

Dacron double-braid rope can be given a more comfortable *hand* by adding spun polyester to the outer cover. This type of rope does not wear as well as conventional Dacron double braid, but it is easier on the crew's hands when hauling on sailboat sheets or halyards. Dacron ropes for sailboats are often dyed in bright reds, blues, and greens to allow for color coding.

A small amount of three-strand twist rope is made from Dacron fiber. This rope allows owners of traditional sailing craft to enjoy the benefits of no-stretch halyards and sheets without compromising appearance.

Polypropylene

Strength: Moderate
Stretch: Low
Construction: Plaited, occasionally double braid
Primary Uses: Ski tow rope; dinghy painter; towing
Cost: Low

Raw material for this fiber is also a by-product of oil refining. Filaments are produced by melt spinning, after which they are stretched to control elasticity and breaking strength. Under moderate amounts of stretch, polypropylene quickly recovers its original length. Its stretch characteristics and strength are the same wet or dry.

A low melting point is a major drawback. Polypropylene begins to soften at 155 degrees C and melts at 165 degrees C. This characteristic may be a major factor in the relatively low chafe resistance exhibited by rope made of this material. Exposure to strong sunlight also hastens the chemical breakdown of polypropylene. For these reasons, poly rope is not suggested for anchoring or mooring where the vessel will be unattended for extended periods of time.

The specific gravity of polypropylene is less than that of water, so poly rope floats. This makes it attractive for dinghy painters or tow ropes because it will not sink and become entangled in the propeller of the towing vessel. Being lightweight, poly ropes are much easier to handle than ropes of equal strength made from other fibers.

Kevlar

Strength: Exceptional
Stretch: Nil
Construction: Double braid
Primary Use: Sailboat running rigging
Cost: Extremely high

Kevlar is a space-age fiber for the cost-is-no-object sailboat racing group. Individual fibers are famous for being "stronger than steel" on a pound-for-pound basis. Kevlar rope has virtually no stretch under load, which allows precise sail control. Unfortunately, Kevlar fibers within the rope cut or abrade each other. Worse, if pulled around a sharp bend (like a small sheave), they break. These characteristics seriously reduce the working life of Kevlar rope. An even more unfortunate characteristic of pure Kevlar rope is its astronomically high cost.

Combining it with other fibers is one way to get Kevlar's advantages while reducing its drawbacks. A typical combination is Dacron and Kevlar in a 50:50 ratio. Dacron gives the rope abrasion resistance and the ability to work through standard-size sheaves without breaking. Kevlar virtually eliminates stretch. Combination rope of this ratio stretches less than 1 percent of its length at a load equal to 15 percent of its breaking strength.

Low-stretch rope is critical to racing sailors because it allows precise sail control.

HANDLING SYNTHETIC ROPE

Synthetic fibers do not rot, nor are they subject to structural damage from mildew. Rope made of synthetics can be stored wet, although this practice is not recommended. Moisture from wet rope may permeate the rest of the boat and provide a perfect environment for mildew on bedding and upholstery. Instead of storing wet rope, fake it down on deck in the sun for an hour or so. This should allow it to dry sufficiently to send below safely.

Coiling and Storage

Coiling rope is a seaman's art. Nothing marks you as a lubber more than wrapping a line into a tight bundle around your arm. Learning how to coil rope correctly takes only a few seconds. Beginners are always surprised to learn that coiling is one job where doing it the right way is also doing it the easy way.

TWISTED ROPE

(Right-hand lay) Pick up the line in your left hand. Let it lie in your palm with the left thumb pointing away from the body. Gather in clockwise loops of rope with your right hand. As each loop is laid into your left hand, impart a slight half twist with

Twisted rope is coiled *clockwise*. Right-handers gather rope with their right hand and lay the coils into their left. Note the position of the bitter end (eye splice) in this illustration.

the right thumb and forefinger. Roll the rope away from your body. This produces neat coils that lie quietly in the left hand. Unfortunately, the twists imparted into the rope to make it coil smoothly may cause hockles when it is paid out. More on this problem later.

BRAIDED ROPE

Imparting a half twist to make the coils lie flat should not be done with braided rope. Just lay the coils into your left hand without half rolls between the right thumb and forefinger. Without these twists, the loops will be large figure eights instead of neat ovals. However, the line will pay out smoothly despite its untidy appearance. If half twists are put into a braided line, it becomes a self-tangling mess when paid out.

THE "UN-COIL"

Braided or twisted rope can be made to lie in neat loops through a coiling process involving alternate-direction loops. The first loop is taken as a conventional clockwise overhand loop with a half twist. The second loop is taken under-handed and counterclockwise. Grasp the incoming line with the *back* of the coiling hand toward your body. As you pull in the bight, rotate your

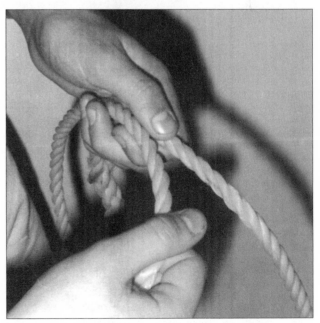

The first loop of an "un-coil" is taken in the standard manner for coiling three-strand rope. A half twist is rolled into the loop to make it lie quietly in the hand.

hand up and toward you to lay a reverse loop in the holding hand. Done correctly, the second loop is coiled in the opposite direction from the first. Continue with alternate overhand forward and underhand backward loops until the line is coiled.

Each overhand or backward loop imparts a half twist into the rope. However, they are in opposite directions, so the half twists cancel each other when the line pays out. This prevents the formation of hockles because the line runs out without twisting.

Sometimes no amount of twisting or coiling tricks can coax a line to lie in neat loops. This is often true of rope that has recently been under load and has not "relaxed" back to its original length. Double-braid rope sometimes responds

The second loop of an "un-coil" is taken underhanded and counterclockwise. The loop is formed in the opposite direction to the standard manner of coiling rope. Note the position of the right hand as it lays the second loop into the left hand.

well to being coiled backward, that is, counterclockwise. This seems to help reorient the inner and outer sennits so that the rope behaves better. Sterner measures are needed with three-strand or particularly recalcitrant braided rope.

Dragging a length of rope behind the boat is the traditional (and still best) method of relaxing it. Secure one end to a stern quarter cleat before carefully sending the entire length over the taffrail. The boat should move forward to prevent the rope from tangling with the propellers. A speed of four to six knots works best. High speeds should be avoided.

Drag the rope for at least fifteen minutes. Water flowing along its length massages the individual fibers of the rope back into their original orientations. Slow the boat to bare steerageway to lighten the job of hauling the line back on board. Minimal way keeps the line streaming away from both the boat and the propellers. Stop the rotation of the propellers while the last thirty to fifty feet are brought in. Fake the line on deck until it dries enough to be coiled and sent below.

Safety Note

Caution must always be observed when towing lines astern. Damage to the rope, propeller, or driveshaft will result if the rope tangles with machinery. Personal injuries to the person coiling the line may also occur. Never stand in loops or bights of rope at any time or put wraps of rope around your hands when handling a line towed astern or when coiling the line back aboard.

END UNRAVELING

A rope doesn't want to unweave or untwist unless it is subject to some trauma—like being cut off a spool. Cut ends begin to unravel almost immediately. The generic term for the various methods of preventing this is *whipping*. In the old days, whippings were always made of waxed or tarred "small stuff." Today, purists continue to tie or sew this type of whipping on their ropes, although other, high-tech methods are available.

Heat Sealing

Most chandlers use a hot knife to cut synthetic rope. The heat of the blade melts the individual fibers into a solid bead of nylon or Dacron. A well-made bead effectively prevents the rope from fraying or unraveling. Unfortunately, many store clerks do little more than slice through the rope and hand it to the customer. A few fibers are melted together in the process, but not enough to provide a long-lasting whipping. The best way to achieve a proper sealing yourself is to rotate the end of the rope slowly over an open flame until the fibers coalesce. Then, let the bead of molten nylon cool naturally.

The resulting bead is usually larger in diameter than the rope, so it may not go through blocks or fairleads. If caution is observed, a cool knife may be used to shape the molten fiber, although this technique can create as many problems as it solves.

Safety Warning

Molten nylon, Dacron, or polypropylene can cause severe burns if allowed to drip on the flesh. Safety gloves and goggles are advised. Never hold the rope over any part of your body. Do not touch the fused end for several minutes, as melted fiber retains heat. Always keep children away from flames and hot fiber.

Rope End Dip

Rope end dip is a quick-drying liquid plastic that prevents fraying by sealing the fibers. Either dip the cut end of the rope into the plastic or brush the material into the fibers of the rope. Wait a few min-

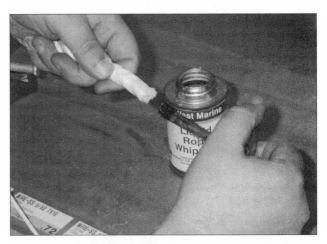

Using liquid plastic rope end dip is an easy way of whipping a rope. The rope can be dipped, or the plastic brushed onto the surface of the rope as is being done here.

utes for it to cure. This type of chemical whipping is relatively long-lasting, but can be damaged or peeled off by abuse over time. The hardened plastic end may not go through sheaves or fairleads because it is slightly larger in diameter than the rope. While not a traditional method, dipping the ends of a rope is quick and relatively permanent. Also, it has few of the dangers of melting with heat.

Shrink Wrap

Electronic technicians have been protecting wire splices with heat-shrinkable tubing for years. Short sections of this special tubing can also be pushed over the end of a rope, and then heated with a heat gun. The tubing reacts to the heat by shrinking tightly around the rope. Shrink-wrapped ends are extremely durable, and the tubing comes in various colors for coding the various ropes on board.

Rigging Tape

A quick way of whipping the ends of a rope is with synthetic rubber rigging tape. Made of a special rubber compound, this tape adheres to itself when stretched. Mariner's Choice, one manufacturer, claims its brand of tape will bond even when dirty or wet. Temperatures from -5 degrees to 250 degrees F have no effect on it. Once bonded, it will not peel with age the way glue-based tapes do. Self-adhering rigging tape comes in either black or white and is one inch wide.

True Whippings

True old-fashioned whippings are made with waxed twine. The best is flat twine heavily impregnated with beeswax, but this is often impossible to find. Hard, round twine that is lightly filled with beeswax is usually readily available.

Use rigging tape to quickly whip the end of a rope. Use the tape made of special rubber that adheres to itself. Do not use sticky tape as it will become gummy and peel off in hot weather.

(Courtesy Mariner's Choice)

If neither of these can be found locally, ordinary synthetic fiber twine can be used by rubbing it across a cake of beeswax several times. Waxing the twine makes it stickier so the whipping stays in place longer. It also gives some protection against chemical damage and mechanical wear. When you are sewing canvas, the wax lubricates the hole through which the twine must be pulled.

Each wrap of a whipping is pulled tightly around the rope and placed right next to the previous one. An old bosun's rule of thumb is that the wrapped area should be equal in length to the diameter of the rope. Sloppy wrapping is the main cause of failed whippings. The twine should be wrapped in the *opposite* direction from the lay of the rope. Work slowly and pull continuously on the twine as you wrap it around the rope. Flat twine seems to have more friction, so it is less likely to unwrap if you let the tension loose. The wraps of flat twine can also be overlapped very slightly to increase their holding power. Wraps of round twine must be laid right next to one another.

COMMON WHIPPING

This method is intended for temporary or light duty only. A bight of twine slightly longer than the diameter of the line is laid against the rope and held in place by the first turn of the whipping. Later turns are built on top of this bight until the whipping achieves the desired length. The working end of the twine is fed through the original

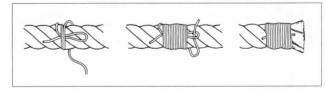

A common whipping is done with waxed twine. A bight of twine is laid against the rope and captured with the wrappings. The end of the twine is taken through this bight, which is then pulled under the wrappings. Loose ends are trimmed off.

bight, which is then pulled back under the wraps of the whipping. Excess twine is trimmed away.

SAILMAKER'S WHIPPING

This method takes longer and requires waxed twine, a sailor's palm, and a sailmakers needles, but usually outlasts the working life of the rope.

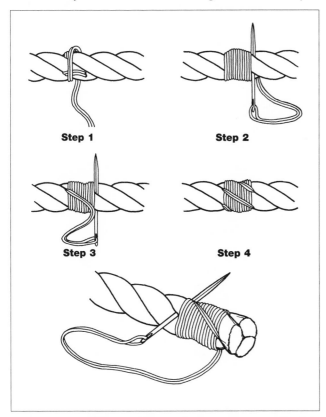

Step 1

Step 2

Step 3

Step 4

A sailmaker's whipping requires waxed twine and a needle. The twine is sewn through the rope, then wrapped tightly around its circumference. Stitches are then taken along the grooves in the rope. A final stitch is taken through the center of the rope and loose ends are trimmed off.

The twine is first "sewn" through the rope using a needle. Pull all but a small length through before beginning the wraps. This stub end of twine is covered by the whipping. When the appropriate length of rope has been whipped, the twine is again sewn through the rope, but this time the point of the needle emerges in the groove between two strands at one end of the whipping. Follow that groove to the other end of the whipping and sew it through again, forcing the needle out in a different groove. Repeat the process until all three grooves are filled, take one final stitch through the rope, and cut off excess twine.

BASIC KNOTS

Don't tie yourself in knots over knots!

There's no need to be an old shellback just to tie up a boat or hang fenders properly. Over the years, the simple skill of tying knots has become something of a mystic art known as *marlinespike seamanship*. Fear of the mysteries of carrick bends or Spanish bowlines has caused people to drop out of safe-boating classes. It's a shame, because there's nothing mysterious or difficult about using knots successfully.

One of the first mysteries to dispel concerns the terms *bends*, *hitches*, and *knots*. Old-time sailors generally agreed that a *bend* was used to connect two ropes together, a *knot* tied the rope to itself, and a *hitch* connected a rope to a fixed object like a bollard or cleat. Today it's permissible to use the general term *knot* in all cases.

Some traditional terms cannot be dealt with so casually, however. In order to communicate it's necessary to use nautical words that may not be familiar (see box, page 14).

Knots work by causing the rope to jam against itself. Friction and the pull of the load keep the knot tight. Good knots have one cardinal virtue: they can be untied. "Hatchet knots" that need a fire ax to open are the mark of sloppy seamen. Owing to rather sophisticated physics, knots are never as strong as the rope in which they are

Marlinespike Terminology

- **Bight**—the portion of the rope in which the knot is tied. Also, the loop of rope formed by tying a knot. In general use, any U-shaped, open loop of rope.

- **Bitter End**—the end of a rope farthest from the anchor. This is the end that should be attached to the boat. If it is not, a bitter lesson is learned.

- **Fall**—the same as the lazy end.

- **Lazy End**—the portion of the rope between the knot (e.g., on a deck cleat) and the actual bitter end.

- **Round Turn**—a wrap and a half taken around any object such as a piling or bollard so that the lazy end comes off the piling parallel to the working end, heading back toward the load.

- **Standing End**—the main portion of the rope, usually the part toward the load. Also known as the working end.

- **Turn**—a single wrap around any object such as a piling or bollard so that the lazy end comes off in line with the working end and going away from the load.

- **Working End**—see Standing End.

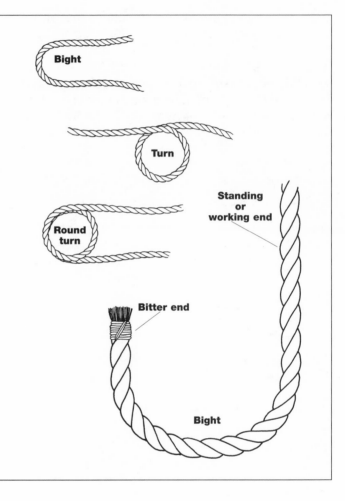

tied. They always cause some fibers to be stretched while others are crushed under strain from the load. Even the best knots reduce the strength of the rope, sometimes by 50 percent.

Splices are stronger than knots because they work on the same twisting or weaving principles as the construction of the rope. Table 1-5 shows the strength of selected knots and splices compared with the strength of the rope.

Table 1-5

Strength Lost to Knots and Splices	
KNOT OR SPLICE	PERCENTAGE OF ORIGINAL STRENGTH
Cleat Hitch	60–65%
Two Half Hitches	70%
Clove Hitch	60%
Bowline	60%
Eye Splice	93%
Short Splice	85%

KNOT MODULES

Everything from electronics to multistory buildings is constructed of "modules" these days. In keeping with this modern trend toward modularity, the basic underhand loop that forms most knots can be described as a "knot module." It's formed by taking the lazy end *under* the standing part to form a loop (properly called an "underhand turn"). Depending upon how this basic knot module is applied, it can become part of a clove hitch, two half hitches, or more complicated knots. Learning to combine basic knot modules into working knots constitutes the bulk of marlinespike seamanship for modern boating.

The knot module is a simple underhand loop. It is the basis for the majority of the knots used in modern boating.

Clove Hitch and Half Hitches

CLOVE HITCH
This knot is used to fasten a rope to a fixed object. Typically, this knot is "thrown" around a dock riser when tying up a boat. Start a clove hitch by making an underhand turn (our module) large enough in diameter to drop over the riser. Make a second underhand turn and drop it over the riser above the

first. Tighten the knot by pulling on the lazy end with one hand while straightening the loops with the other. Some people can tie a clove hitch in midair, then drop it over the piling and draw the knot tight with one hand. Mere mortals tie this knot one module at a time to avoid tangles.

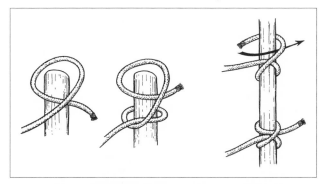

A clove hitch is used to tie a line to a bollard or piling. It consists of two underhand loops (knot modules) stacked on top of each other.

When it's done correctly, the standing part and lazy end of a clove hitch come off the piling or bollard in opposite directions. If the lazy end comes off the knot *toward* the load, the second turn was made overhand instead of underhand. This results in a weaker knot that is likely to slip.

TWO HALF HITCHES
Instead of tying the rope to a piling, this knot is tied around its own standing part. Although it is similar to a clove hitch, the resulting knot is known as *two half hitches*. (No, two half hitches are *not* called a "whole hitch.") Tying two half hitches creates a running loop that is adjustable in size. If tied around a spar pole or piling, this loop tightens as the knot comes under strain.

It's obvious now that a knot module is really just a half hitch. Single half hitches are seldom used because they have little holding power and come apart as soon as the rope goes slack.

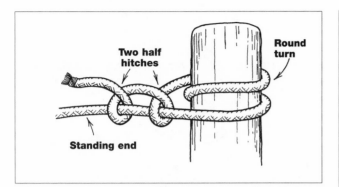

A round turn and two half hitches are the preferred method for securing to a piling. The round turn is taken first, then the half hitches. Although quickly done, this is an excellent way of securing a line for long-term dockage.

However, put two of them together and the result is a most useful knot, especially for docking.

The standard way of using half hitches when mooring a boat is in conjunction with a round turn on a piling or riser. The round turn absorbs the load, making it easier to tie the knot. It also keeps the strain on the working part from drawing the half hitches so tight that fingers can't untie them. After taking a round turn, secure the rope with two half hitches around its standing part.

Knowing when to use a clove hitch or when to take a round turn and two half hitches is more art than science. A clove hitch is easily tied, but it can loosen if the load comes off the standing part. On the other hand, this knot can become nearly impossible to untie if subjected to continuous loading. For these reasons the clove hitch is usually reserved for temporary duty.

Need to hang a fender from a stainless steel railing? A round turn and two half hitches does the job. If the fender wants to "ride" fore or aft along the rail, try taking two or three additional round turns before making the hitches. Extra turns provide increased friction on the rail to keep the fender in position.

ANCHOR BEND

Sometimes called *fisherman's bend*, this is a highly specialized version of the round turn and two half hitches. Before it was common to use a section of chain in anchor rodes, the rope was tied directly to a ring or shackle at the end of the anchor shank. This knot was developed to do the job and to not untie itself while lying on the bottom.

Start by taking two turns through the ring. Leave these a little loose so the bitter end can be passed *through* them before continuing the knot. Draw the turns tight after passing the bitter end through. Then take two or more half hitches around the standing part of the rope. An extra half hitch (or two) gives a bit more feeling of security, although it shouldn't be needed. While

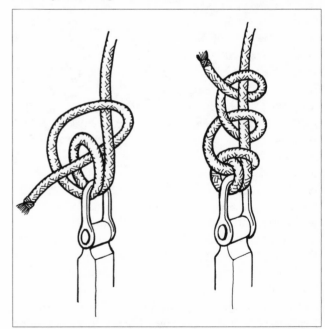

An anchor bend is closely related to the round turn and two half hitches. The knot is started by taking two turns through the ring or shackle with the bitter end tucked through them. The turns are snugged and two (or more) half hitches taken above them.

this knot is seldom used on anchors these days, it does come in handy occasionally. It's excellent for securing a line to the steel rings or eyes commonly found on piers or floating catwalks.

Cleat Hitch

Knot experts consider the cleat hitch a separate knot. But look closely. A cleat hitch is built upon our familiar knot module. The finished hitch closely resembles a clove hitch taken around the horns of the cleat. The configuration is slightly different from securing to a dock piling, but the basic knot works in the same manner.

The mistake most people make when securing a line on a cleat is forgetting to wrap a bight around the base of the cleat to spread the strain. Without this wrap, all of the strain comes on one horn of the cleat, which might fail. Or the horn may chafe enough to cause the rope to break.

Begin a cleat hitch by leading the standing part under the end of the horn farthest from the load. For descriptive purposes, this will be the "first horn" of the cleat. Bring the rope under the first horn, then wrap a bight around the side of the base away from the load and then under the second horn. This creates the often-overlooked bight around the base.

Next, wrap the line over the top of the center of the cleat. Using a figure-eight motion, bring it back under the first horn. Continue the figure-eight motion to take the line over the center and back under the second horn. No more than two figure-eight wraps should be needed. Beginners put far too many turns on, with no result other than creating an ugly bird's nest.

Cleat hitches are finished in two different ways, depending upon their use. If the line is being secured permanently (as in a long-term docking), the hitch is finished with an underhand loop (a knot module) over the first horn. This

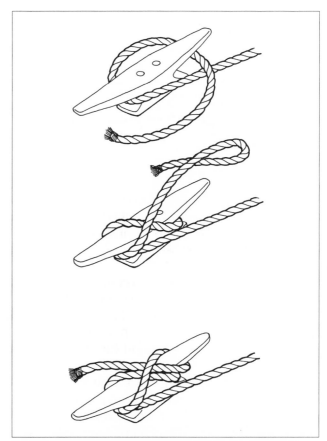

A cleat hitch starts by taking a turn around the base of the cleat. Figure-eight loops are taken over the cleat horns. The hitch is finished with a half hitch over one horn.

locks the lazy end under itself and prevents the cleat hitch from slipping under load. On sailboats it's often necessary to release a cleated line quickly. In this case, the cleat hitch is finished by taking a round turn under both horns and around the base.

It would be ideal if we could go on this way forever, building new knots on the basic knot module. Unfortunately, reality doesn't work that way. A knot of completely different construction is needed to complete a knot-tying education.

"The Knot King": The Bowline

The bowline is unique, and it's absolutely necessary to know. Called the king of knots, it can be used to create a loop in the end of a rope, to secure a line to a deck fitting, or to join two ropes together. A bowline simply can't untie itself, yet one that has been under hundreds of pounds of strain can be easily untied. About the only thing that can't be done with a bowline is untying it under load.

Some show-offs know the theatrical trick of tying a bowline one-handed. An old salt working 150 feet off the deck on a clipper ship yard hanging on with one hand needed to know how to tie this knot with his one free hand. Modern boating seldom demands a one-handed performance of the bowline (or any other knot). All that's required is to learn the plain and simple two-handed way.

Start with the rope in the left hand. The standing part should loop over the top of the left index finger and drop to the floor with the lazy end lying across your palm. Using the right hand, make a small *overhand* loop in your left palm. Hold that loop in position with your left thumb.

Bring the lazy end through the loop from the back side. Push the end of the rope through from back to front. This produces a bight, which can be adjusted in size to suit the need. Pull enough of the bitter end through the loop to take it around *behind* the standing part. Finish the knot by sending the bitter end back through the loop and pulling everything tight.

The size of the working bight (or *eye*) created by the bowline must be regulated as the knot is tied. After you've finished, the eye can't be changed without breaking the knot and tying a new one. Be sure to thread the lazy end through any shackles, rings, or pad eyes before making the knot.

A bowline is "broken" by pushing on the bight that holds the bitter end while at the same time

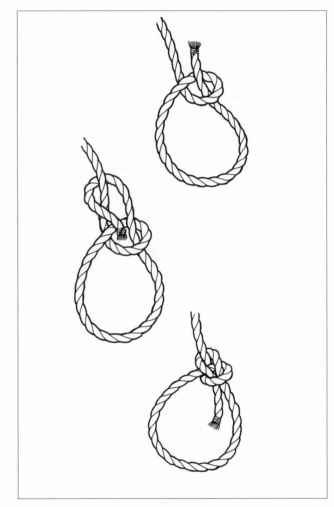

The bowline starts with an overhand loop. Push the bitter end up through this loop and around behind the standing part. Bring the bitter end back down through the loop and draw the knot tight. The size of the working bight must be adjusted before the knot is finished.

pushing on the standing part of the line. Wiggle things a bit and eventually the knot will loosen up enough to be untied. How long it takes to break a bowline depends upon the load to which it was subjected. A fid may be necessary to work things loose if the knot has been under heavy strain.

Sailor Knots

Sailing has always been a game of "pulling strings." Halyards, sheets, guys, topping lifts, and reef lines all depend upon rope to function. This means that sailors must know a few additional knots:

STOPPER KNOT

Also known as a *figure eight*, this knot is primarily used to keep sheets from running away through blocks or fairleads. Make an overhand loop in the end of the rope. Then dip the bitter end underneath the standing portion and pull it through the loop. Tighten the knot on itself.

For a figure eight or stopper knot, make an overhand loop, dip the bitter end behind the standing part, pull the end through the loop, and tighten.

REEF KNOT

Also known as a *square knot*, it is excellent for lashing furled sails (hence the *reef* name) or tying the string on a package. A square knot should never be used to tie two lines together. Almost everyone has heard the old bromide for tying this knot, "Right over left, then left over right."

ROLLING HITCH

This knot allows a smaller line to be secured to the working part of a larger line. Useful for applying tension to a sheet when removing riding turns from a winch. Also used by catamaran

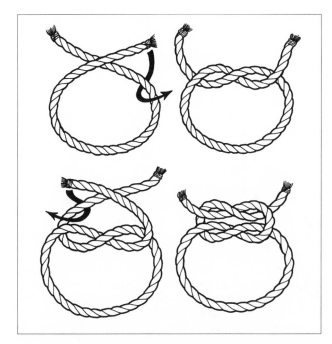

The rule for tying a reef (or square) knot is "right over left, then left over right." Note the symmetry of the completed knot.

sailors to make an anchor bridle. A rolling hitch is really just a clove hitch with an extra turn in the middle. It will slide one way (but not the

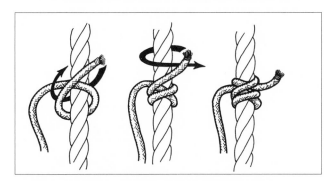

A rolling hitch starts by taking two turns around the hawser. Each of these turns captures the standing portion of the rope. A half hitch is then made above the two turns to secure the knot. A rolling hitch will slide one way along the hawser, but not the other.

other) along the larger line to which it is tied.

There are hundreds more knots, each with a specific use and with its own fan club. At the risk of offending the fans of more obscure knots, the ones listed above are the basic knots that sailors should know. There is no need to make things any more complicated. However, if winters are long and you have a spare piece of rope lying about, the search for new knots can be an intriguing hobby.

Practice Knot Tying

At this point you may want to hunt up a piece of practice line. Knot tying is like riding a horse—you have to learn by doing, you can't just read about it. The best rope for practice is ³⁄₈-inch manila, although it can be difficult to obtain these days. Substitute a hard lay ³⁄₈-inch twisted nylon. This diameter is large enough to fit comfortably in the hand. Don't try to learn knots on anything bigger than ¹⁄₂-inch-diameter rope. Larger rope is simply too stiff. It fights knots, making the learning process miserable. You'll need a practice rope about ten feet long.

Knots You Don't Need

There are a few knots or bends that appear in nearly every book on marlinespike seamanship yet are useless on a modern pleasure boat. Among them are the:

- **Sheepshank**—Every Boy Scout learns this knot, which claims to shorten a line without cutting it. Unfortunately, it is famous for coming apart on its own, especially if the strain is not continuous. It's much safer to use one end of a long line and coil up the unused portion.

- **Granny Knot**—This is the knot most people tie when they intend a reef or square knot. Most of the time it unties itself, but on occasion it jams into the ultimate hatchet knot.

- **Carrick Bend**—Recommended for tying two ropes together, this knot works best on ropes of larger diameter than commonly found on pleasure boats. Two interlocking bowlines are more secure and take only a few seconds longer to tie.

Basic Splices

Learning to splice is not difficult. Most people can get the knack of putting an eye splice in twisted rope with only minimal practice. Splicing braided rope takes more concentration. (Everyone has to read the instructions every time.) Splicing a set of dock lines does more than just provide the satisfaction of doing a job. It also saves money. Do-it-yourself lines cost up to a third less than those that are factory-spliced.

THREE-STRAND TWISTED LAY

Start by counting fourteen to sixteen "crowns," or twists, from the bitter end. Put a wrap of ordinary

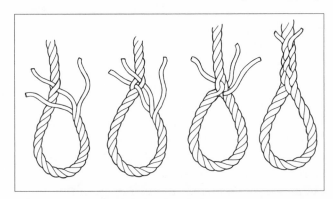

Splicing an eye in twisted rope is simple. Step 1: Unlay the bitter end and tuck the middle strand under one crown of the standing part. Step 2: Tuck the inside strand over the next crown. Note that it goes over the crown under which the first tuck was taken. Step 3: Turn the rope over and take a third tuck using the remaining strand. This tuck is taken under the crown from right to left. Pull tight. At least three rounds of tucks should be taken in natural fiber and four in synthetic rope.

½-inch masking tape around the rope to mark this spot. Determine the size of the completed eye and mark this spot on the standing portion with another wrap of tape. Unlay the bitter end to the first wrap of tape. (Hint: You can prevent the unlaid strands from unraveling by wrapping them with tape.)

With the standing portion going up over the top of your hand, form the eye by bending the bitter end to the right. Marry the standing part and bitter ends. Take the middle unlaid strand and push it under the first twist above the second wrap of tape. Pull tight. Next, take the *inside* (bottom) unlaid strand over the first twist and under the twist lying immediately to its left around the rope. Pull tight.

Turn the eye over to make the third tuck. Take the remaining strand under its twist. Be sure to take this tuck from *right to left* as shown in the drawings. All three strands should now come out of the twists of the standing part in a horizontal band around the rope. Each strand should go under one twist. All strands should be separated by one twist from each other.

Continue the splice by taking a series of three tucks using each of the strands. (In marlinespike terminology, each round is called a *tuck*.) A minimum of three tucks should be taken in natural- and four in synthetic-fiber rope. Pull each strand tight after every tuck. Most splicers take at least one additional tuck "for good measure." Extra tucks do no harm and may prevent the splice from failing under strain.

Tapering is an elegant way of finishing an eye splice. Take an additional round of tucks using only two of the three strands. Then, take another tuck with just one of the two remaining strands. Tapering adds little strength to the splice, but greatly improves its appearance.

Use a sharp knife to trim off excess length of the strands. Don't cut them flush with the body of

the rope. Leave about ¼ to ⅜ inch sticking out. Seal the ends of the strand with a hot knife or a match. (These ends will pull into the rope when it is put under load.) After the molten fiber cools, roll the splice in your hands or under your foot to give it a smooth, round appearance.

SINGLE BRAID

The most common hollow single-braid rope is polypropylene. Because of its extremely slippery nature, eye splices in poly rope need extra length for security. Even so, they are less trustworthy than splices in nylon or Dacron rope. Start by measuring up from the bitter end a distance of about twenty times the rope's diameter. Mark this location. Form the eye and make a corresponding mark on the standing portion next to the first mark on the bitter end.

Use a fid to poke a hole through the standing portion at the second mark. Push the bitter end through this hole until the first mark is flush with the outside of the standing portion. Creating an opening large enough is not difficult if you have a splicing fid. Count up three pairs of strands (about one diameter of the rope) and push the bitter end back through the standing portion. Continue "sewing" the bitter end through the standing part until all but two inches of the bitter end are used up. Insert this tail into the center of the standing portion. Push it through an opening in one side of the standing part.

An alternative technique requires a plastic splicing fid designed for this type of rope. Take just two stitches through the standing portion. Then, use the fid to insert the bitter end inside the standing part. It helps to "milk" the standing portion toward the splice to increase its diameter.

With either type of splice, you can add extra strength by lock stitching the throat of the eye with waxed twine. The throat is the place where the bitter end marries the standing part to form the eye.

DOUBLE BRAID

A variety of methods are available to splice double-braid rope. All require proprietary tools, usually described as *fids*. Each of these tools comes with an illustrated set of instructions. Spread the instructions on your worktable and go to work. Follow each step exactly as described to produce an excellent splice.

2

ANCHORS, RODES, AND DECK GEAR

Equipment that goes into the water when anchoring—the anchor, chain, shackles, and rope—is collectively known as *ground tackle*. While the anchor gets most of the credit for doing the work, it can only be successful when combined with the other members of the ground tackle team.

The U.S. Coast Guard does not require American boats to carry anchors. However, many of the states do mandate that boats operating on their waters have at least one anchor aboard. Despite these state laws, few pleasure boats are functionally equipped to anchor in heavy weather or under emergency conditions. Just having an anchor and rode aboard isn't enough. The ground tackle package must be suited to the boat and stored in such a manner that it can be deployed quickly.

People who are willing to spend hundreds of thousands of dollars on their floating homes will scrimp when purchasing anchors and line. The problem is worse among the powerboat fraternity than among sailors, although neither group is immune. Inadequate ground tackle is probably the reason behind the erroneous belief that anchoring is a difficult and uncertain process. This is a sad state of affairs because the ability to anchor can add so much enjoyment to the ownership of a boat. Anglers drop the hook to hold their position above a "hot spot." Nothing beats anchoring in a secluded spot to swim off the boat on a lazy summer afternoon. And anyone who has done any extended cruising knows that spending the night on the hook in a protected cove is one of life's great pleasures.

ANCHOR DESIGNS

The earliest known anchors were little more than forked tree limbs weighted with rocks and tied to ropes. More than likely, the weight of the rock did most of the anchoring, although the forked branch might occasionally hook into something on the sea bottom and provide additional security. Known as a *killik*, this type of crude anchor still survives on native craft in some areas of the world. Not much changed in anchor design until the beginning of the Iron Age. Iron is heavy enough that it doesn't need rock ballast. Someone quickly figured out that an iron anchor with two opposed arms had a better chance of hooking into the bottom than a one-armed anchor. Adding a wooden crossmember made sure that one of the arms was always pointing into the ground. The pattern thus developed for the traditional stock anchor has remained basically unchanged for more than two thousand years.

Anchors of traditional design have been traced back as far as the Roman Empire. In 1931, two ships dated from the reign of the Roman emperor Caligula were discovered on the bottom of Italy's Lake Nemi. Aboard one of those was a thirteen-foot-long iron anchor not significantly different from smaller versions available today. Of course, the stock anchor of antiquity has been supplanted on today's popularity list by modern

The design of traditional ships' anchors has not changed in more than two thousand years. This traditional anchor is on a New England schooner. A similar pattern is used today for some yacht anchors.

designs that are lighter in weight and easier to handle. Today's pleasure boat anchors fall into five broad categories:

STOCK-IN-HEAD

By far the most popular of this style anchor is the original design developed by Danforth (1939) under its trade name. Many companies now produce similar-design anchors, although the performance of the imitators may vary widely from the original World War II design. Often called *patent anchors*, they are available in galvanized steel and corrosion-resistant aluminum.

Lightweight stock-in-head anchors are favored aboard most U.S. pleasure boats. They are based on a design originated by Danforth during World War II. Most are made of galvanized steel, but this Fortress anchor is aluminum. *(Courtesy Nav-X)*

PLOW STYLE

The original CQR anchor (1933) looks much like a horse-drawn farm plow, from which the type gets its name. This type of anchor was invented in the United Kingdom.

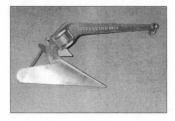

Plow anchors originated in the United Kingdom under the CQR brand name. True plows like this one look much like a horse-drawn farm implement and are made of heavy forgings.

In the 1970s, the Bruce anchor was developed for holding oil rigs in the turbulent North Sea. Although a CQR looks much like a farm plow, the Bruce has the appearance of a manta ray on steroids.

The Bruce anchor is a refinement of plow-style designs. It was developed for anchoring oil rigs in the North Sea. *(Courtesy Bruce)*

STOCK ANCHORS

These are the traditional anchors from antiquity. Known today as a *yachtsman*, or *Herreshoff pattern* anchor, most such anchors feature a folding stock that remains captive to the shank for convenient stowage.

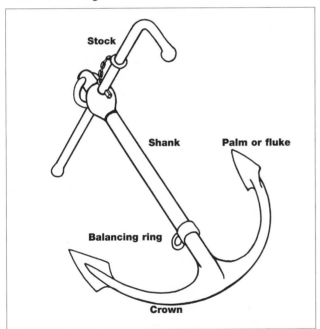

Traditional anchors are known as yachtsman or Herreshoff pattern today. The names for parts of all anchors are taken from this style anchor.

MUSHROOMS

Such anchors get their name from their shape, which is somewhat reminiscent of an upside-down toadstool. In small sizes these are the favorites of anglers, while larger ones are used for permanent moorings.

Mushroom anchors get their name from their appearance. Small ones are used by anglers while larger versions serve as permanent moorings.

GRAPNELS

Folding versions are popular as dinghy anchors. Grapnels with fixed prongs are also used for retrieving objects lost on the bottom. In this use they are often known as *grappling hooks*.

Deliberately left off this list are the so-called Navy pattern anchors that are miniature versions of big ship anchors. They have no stocks and wide, fat flukes. Although the appearance of these anchors inspires confidence, it is mis-

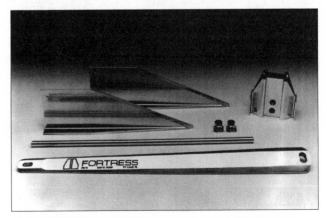

Lightweight aluminum Fortress anchors are easily disassembled for stowage. This is a handy feature in cramped quarters, but reassembly delays quick deployment in an emergency.
(Courtesy Nav-X)

placed. Navy pattern anchors rely almost entirely upon weight for their holding ability. The flukes do little, if any, work. A functional anchor of this type for a thirty-footer weighs more than the average man can comfortably lift.

Stock-in-head anchors such as the original Danforth use scientifically shaped flukes made of formed sheet metal in place of cast iron bulk. Some, like the Fortress anchors, are made of aluminum, proving that weight plays a minimal part in their performance. Low cost and light weight have made stock-in-head anchors the most popular for U.S. boats. Their relatively flat design allows easy storage in an anchor locker or in a bracket on a lifeline stanchion. These anchors work well in sand, clay, or similar bottom conditions, where their holding ability is legendary. (Danforth anchors were used to pull the battleship *Missouri* off the sand when it went aground after World War II.)

Don't Modify Danforth Stocks

Although it can be a nuisance, don't shorten the tubular steel stock of a true Danforth anchor. The long Danforth stock likes to catch everything from dock lines to the captain's toes. Almost everyone who has owned one of these anchors has had the temptation to reduce the length of the offending piece. Don't succumb! While the length of the stock can make handling and storage cumbersome, it serves an important purpose when the anchor hits the bottom. The long stock forces the Danforth to always land flat, with its flukes positioned for best penetration. Modifying an anchor may seriously compromise its ability to grab on to the bottom.

Plow-style anchors, particularly the authentic CQR brand, have become identification badges for cruising sailboats. Plows have a reputation for holding on all bottoms except smooth rock, where nothing holds. They have even been reported to push their way through thick weeds to bury themselves securely into the bottom. On the negative side, good plow-style anchors are both heavy and cumbersome. They stow properly only on special bow roller fittings. Plows are also among the most expensive anchors to purchase and are not often carried in stock by marine stores.

Stock anchors are still favored in New England because of their ability to penetrate through weeds or to find a place to grab in a rock bottom. (Some skippers call this type of anchor a "rock pick.") On the negative side, a stock anchor is easily fouled by its own rode and is too cumbersome to be handled on most foredecks. Unless it disassembles into several pieces, stowage is virtually impossible aboard a modern boat.

Persnickety sailors claim that only a true Herreshoff pattern stock anchor from the Herreshoff Company foundry should be purchased. Since the company is long out of business, these anchors are extremely rare. Fortunately, an excellent alternative, the Luke Storm Anchor, is widely available. The Luke anchor shares most of the virtues of the Herreshoff design except the famous name. The wide flukes of the Luke anchor dig deeply into rock, clay, kelp, and grass. This anchor breaks down into three pieces for storage.

Mushroom anchors rely primarily upon weight and secondarily upon their ability to sink into the mud on the bottom for their holding ability. Since weight is so important, these anchors quickly grow unmanageable in size. Only the smallest mushrooms can be carried on boats. The time-honored coffee can of concrete found rolling around in the bottom of a johnboat is a crude example of a mushroom fishing anchor. Its job is to hold a small boat more or less in one spot during fair weather. Large mushrooms often weighing a ton or more are used for permanent moorings in anchorages.

How Anchors Penetrate the Bottom

An anchor is a simple device designed to dig into the sea bottom. Connected to the surface by a chain or rope rode, it keeps your boat from drifting under pressure of wind, waves, and current. Each part of the anchor plays a role in the process. The flukes do the actual work of digging into the bottom, while the stock makes sure the anchor always lands on the bottom with the flukes properly positioned. The shank transmits the pull from the rode into the body of the anchor.

The success of true Danforth brand anchors is based in large part on the specific angle at which the flukes attack the bottom. This angle, the result of careful engineering, is maintained when the anchor hits bottom by the shape of the crown. The plowshare-shaped flukes of a CQR also must attack the bottom at a specific angle for quick, positive penetration. In plows, the attachment of the shank to the plowshare flukes creates this critical angle. Although the correct attack angle for the flukes is engineered into the anchor, in real life this angle may be difficult to achieve or maintain. Many factors involved in the process of anchoring can prevent the anchor from penetrating the bottom at the required angle.

Choosing an Anchor

Seasoned skippers carry two or three different types of anchors to meet different bottom and weather conditions. They know that no single style or brand of anchor is best for all situations of wind, waves, and bottom characteristics. Choosing the right anchor depends upon a careful assessment of many factors:

TYPE OF BOTTOM

Bare rock, sand, broken shells, and soft mud provide completely different holding conditions. A Danforth anchor that works perfectly in sand and is good in shells probably is not your best choice in rock. A stock anchor good for a rocky bottom would offer little help in soft mud. Bottom conditions are the primary factor influencing anchor choice.

SWINGING ROOM

Long scope needed for secure anchoring requires additional swinging room around the anchor. In a crowded anchorage, it may be necessary to choose an anchor that will work with the minimum possible scope.

TYPE OF WEATHER

Storm anchors are always the largest, heaviest, and best-holding anchors aboard. Heavy weather demands ultimate performance from ground tackle. Lighter anchors that are easier to handle are acceptable only in fair weather.

WEATHER CHANGES

Storm fronts are accompanied by major wind shifts. Some anchors, like plows, easily reset themselves after being pulled out of the bottom. Others, like stock-in-head anchors, may not reset themselves. An anchor that easily resets itself is the obvious choice when major wind shifts are expected.

DURATION OF STAY

Anchoring for a couple of hours to swim from the boat or to enjoy a meal calls for a small, light anchor that's easily handled. An overnight stay requires larger, heavier ground tackle.

Anchors should be sized for the job they are to do. A *lunch hook* is a light, easily set anchor suitable only for short duration under ideal weather conditions. The *working anchor* is large enough to hold under moderate weather conditions, including a summer thundershower. A

Table 2-1

Typical Working Anchors*					
BOAT LENGTH	STANDARD DANFORTH	DEEP-SET DANFORTH	CQR PLOW	FORTRESS ALUMINUM	THE BRUCE
Up to 24'	S-600	D-750	20 lb.	FX-7	4.4 lb.
5 to 29'	S-920	D-1150	25 lb.	FX-11	11 lb.
30 to 34'	S-1300	D-1150	25 lb.	FX-16	16.5 lb.
35 to 39'	S-1600	D-1650	35 lb.	FX-16	22 lb.
40 to 44'		D-2000	45 lb.	FX-23	33 lb.
45 to 50'		D-2500	60 lb.	FX-37	44 lb.

*Based on manufacturers' recommendations.

storm anchor (also known as a *sheet anchor*) is the largest carried and is intended for anchoring in the worst of weather or under other difficult conditions.

Table 2-1 is for working anchors only. For storm anchors, increase by two or more sizes, depending upon conditions. No harm is done by putting down an oversize anchor, but boats have been lost by using undersize anchors. Lunch hooks are one or two sizes smaller than working anchors, so it's never safe to leave a boat unattended on one.

How well an anchor holds depends largely upon the type of bottom. From Table 2-2, it's obvious that sand and other fine-grain bottoms provide best holding, while heavy weed growth can make anchoring almost impossible. Table 2-2 is

taken from published manufacturers' data.

Anchor loads generated by wind and waves can be substantial. Wind pressure per square foot of exposed surface increases fourfold every time wind speed doubles. Table 2-3 shows that every square foot of exposed surface (hull, superstructure, masts, and rigging) generates about one third of a pound of wind load at 10 knots wind speed. At 30 knots of wind speed, that load goes up more than tenfold to 3 pounds per square foot.

It's difficult to measure the square footage of your boat that is exposed because it depends on whether the wind is off the bow, off the stern, or at some angle to the side. A much easier way to estimate wind load is to use Table 2-4, which is based on boat length and beam. This table was

Table 2-2

Anchor Choice Based on Type of Bottom						
TYPE OF ANCHOR	SAND	MUD	WEEDS	GRAVEL	ROCK	CORAL
Standard Danforth	VG	VG	P	P	P	P
Deep-Set Danforth	VG	VG	P	P	P	P
CQR Plow	VG	VG	F	G	F	F
Danforth Plow	VG	VG	F	G	F	F
Bruce Anchor	VG	VG	P	G	F	F

VG = Very Good; G = Good; F = Fair; P = Poor

Table 2-3

Wind-Generated Loads	
SPEED (IN KNOTS)	POUNDS PER SQUARE FOOT
10	0.3
20	1.3
30	3.0
40	5.0
50	8.0
60	12.0
100	34.0

prepared by the American Boat and Yacht Council (ABYC) to assist hardware manufacturers and boat builders in estimating expected loads. Enter the table using the boat's overall length (far left column) or the boat's maximum beam (far right column), whichever produces the largest load.

Table 2-4 assumes moderate protection from seas proportionate to hull size. It also assumes freedom for the boat to swing at anchor. You never make a mistake by using a larger anchor

when strong winds or high seas are expected. Storm conditions may require the use of two or more large anchors.

There are no hard-and-fast rules for choosing anchors. The best approach is to use each of your anchors under a variety of conditions. Keep notes on the performance of your anchors in different bottoms and with different amounts of scope. In time, a pattern will develop, indicating which combination of anchor and rode works best for your boat under various conditions.

Is Weight Important?

Cruising sailors almost universally prefer heavy plow-style anchors with long lengths of chain. Yet manufacturers like NAV-X claim their aluminum alloy anchors (sold under the Fortress and Guardian brands) provide superior holding power at a fraction of the weight. Who is right? Or are they both right?

Once an anchor gets down to the bottom, its holding power is almost entirely determined by engineering. An anchor with good design penetrates quickly, buries itself, and holds tenaciously. Nearly all brand-name anchors will get an

Table 2-4

Typical Horizontal Anchor Loads					
WIND SPEED	42 KTS	30 KTS	15 KTS	WIND SPEED	
LENGTH (IN FEET)	STORM ANCHOR	WORKING ANCHOR	LUNCH HOOK	MAXIMUM BEAM (SAIL)	(POWER)
10	320	160	40	4	5
15	500	250	60	6	6
20	720	360	90	7	8
25	980	490	125	8	9
30	1,400	700	175	9	11
35	1,800	900	225	10	13
40	2,400	1,200	30	11	14
50	3,200	1,600	400	13	16
60	4,000	2,000	2,000	15	18

acceptable "bite" if deployed correctly. The real test comes in two other areas. One is the anchor's ability to reset itself if a change in wind or current causes the pull from the boat to come from a different direction. Even more important is the anchor's ability to get down to the bottom in the first place.

Resetting is critical for cruising sailors who often anchor in remote locations where they have little knowledge of local weather patterns. They don't want an overnight wind shift to send their boat dragging onto the rocks. Weight seems to play a factor here. All of the anchors with legendary resetting ability—CQR, Bruce, etc.—are heavy iron or steel castings. Their weight seems to keep them dug into the bottom during the resetting process. (There is little published scientific testing on this subject.) Lightweight anchors seem to pull out of the bottom before they reset, allowing the boat to drag a considerable distance before becoming hooked again.

You would think that a metal anchor of any weight would automatically sink. But some circumstances can prevent a lightweight anchor from ever getting to the bottom. The large, flat flukes of most lightweight anchors can act underwater exactly the same way as the flat paper surfaces of a child's kite do in air. Movement of the boat or a strong current may cause a lightweight anchor to "fly" upward instead of dropping to the bottom. This creates real problems if the boat is drifting rapidly as the result of high winds, waves, or currents. A long length of chain is one tool for forcing a light anchor to drop to the bottom. Once again, weight appears to be the key.

If weight is so important, then, why do Fortress aluminum anchors have such an enviable reputation for performance? The answer to that question goes back to the initial statement that holding power has little to do with the gross weight of the anchor. Fluke angles and other engineering

aspects play the critical roles in determining holding power once the anchor is firmly dug into the bottom. The lighter anchor has another advantage. It is easier to handle on deck and to raise from the deep.

THE ANCHOR RODE

Of equal importance to the anchor is the rode. This is the chain, rope, or wire that connects the anchor to the boat. Most U.S. pleasure boats use a combination rode that includes a short length of chain between the anchor and the nylon rope. A combination rode of this type works better than one made entirely of rope or entirely of chain.

The Rope

Nylon rope is the first choice for anchor rode because it stretches under load. Stretch acts as a shock absorber to "cushion" the boat when it fetches up under the press of wind, current, or waves. Cushioning shock loads makes life aboard the boat more comfortable. More important, it reduces the possibility that the anchor will be jerked out of the bottom. Low-stretch ropes such as Dacron or polypropylene are not suggested for use as an anchor rode because they do not absorb shock loads.

If cost is no object, double-braid nylon rope is

A thimble spliced into the end of an anchor rope protects against chafe. Thimbles may be made of galvanized steel (shown here) or synthetic materials such as nylon.

your best choice because it does not develop torque under load. Three-strand rope may twist under tension if each strand does not share an equal amount of the load. Torque from load twist is transmitted to the bottom, where it tries to upset the anchor. Or the torque may try to untie the rode from its deck cleat. Despite these problems, three-strand nylon is still the overwhelming favorite for anchor rode because it combines favorable stretch characteristics with moderate price. Torque can be minimized by purchasing high-quality rope in which the three strands share the load as equally as possible.

The working end of an anchor rope terminates in an eye splice around a *thimble*. A thimble is an eye-shaped band of galvanized steel or molded nylon designed to prevent the rope from chafing when shackled to the anchor chain. Steel thimbles are always used with natural-fiber rope, but synthetic materials are acceptable with nylon line. The eye splice must be tight around the thimble to keep it in place.

Sailors call the end of the rode farthest from the anchor the *bitter end*. It's a well-chosen name. Forget to secure it and you're sure to learn a bitter lesson as it whips overboard. (Actually, the name bitter end refers to it being the end secured to the bitt.) To prevent losing ground tackle, secure the bitter end to an eye bolt in the anchor locker. U-bolts intended for trailer boat bow eyes work perfectly to secure rodes on boats up to thirty feet. Above that boat size, only a forged eye bolt should be used. Install the eye bolt in the strongest portion of the locker with plenty of backing to spread the strain.

The anchor rode can be tied to the eye bolt with a bowline knot, although knots can be difficult to untie in an emergency. There may come a time when the boat's safety requires slipping the anchor quickly. Cutting the rode loose is the answer. A knife kept permanently in the rope

locker (and sharpened regularly) makes quick work of any knot. More expensive than a knife is attaching a sailboat snap shackle to the eye bolt. Splice an eye *without* a thimble in the bitter end of the rode. The snap shackle holds this eye securely, yet can be popped open even under load. Check the diameter of hawse pipes or fairleads before splicing an eye into the bitter end. These openings may not be large enough to pass the splice.

Although not absolutely necessary, it's helpful to mark the rode at convenient intervals. Marine stores sell markers made of soft plastic for this purpose. Typical sets are numbered for 30, 50, 70, 90, 110, 120, and 150 feet. (The numbers

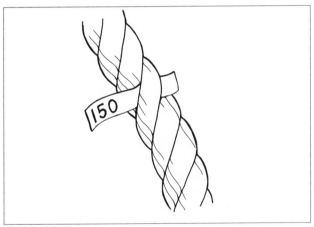

Flexible plastic rode markers are available to indicate the amount of rope sent over the side to the anchor. The markers are threaded between the strands of twisted rope or sewn onto braided rope.

can indicate fathoms or meters as well as feet.) These numbers are intended to be inserted through the lay of three-strand rope. The only way to attach them to braided lines is to sew the plastic to the rope. Indelible felt markers can also be used to mark synthetic rope, although these marks fade quickly.

The Chain

The primary function of chain between the rope and the anchor is to ensure that the pull of the rode on the anchor is as horizontal as possible. A long chain (being heavier) does this job better than a short one. One often-quoted rule of thumb is to have a *minimum* of one foot of chain for every foot of the boat's waterline, or a minimum

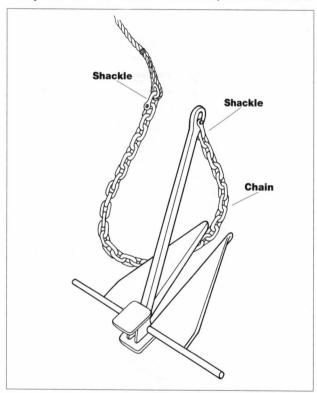

Ground tackle for the typical boat consists of an anchor and fiber rope rode. Shackled between them is a length of chain to improve the anchor's performance. Twisted nylon rope is most popular for the rode, although braided rope is superior.

of fifteen feet. Another rule says to have six feet of chain for every twenty-five feet of water depth. For ease of handling, working anchors often have shorter chains than are recommended by

either rule. However, anything less than six feet of chain is of negligible value. Three types of chain are in general use in the United States: proof coil, BBB, and high test.

PROOF COIL

This is widely used on U.S. farms and in industry. Because of this widespread use, proof coil is the least expensive and easiest-to-purchase form of chain in the United States. Proof-coil chain has a lower-rated safe working strength than high test, but is approximately equal to BBB.

BBB

Triple-B is traditionally preferred for anchor rodes because it weighs more per foot than proof coil. Being heavier, it helps the anchor to hold better than other types of chain. The heavier weight of BBB is the result of more links per foot of chain than proof coil or high test.

HIGH TEST

This is seldom used in anchor rodes because of its greater cost. It is also lighter in weight for any given breaking strength, which can be a disadvantage when anchoring. Using a larger size of proof-coil chain is usually more cost-effective. Larger chain not only achieves the needed strength, but also provides more weight to help the anchor dig into the bottom.

Aside from just weight, chain also serves as a physical insurance policy against chafe. Who knows what's on the bottom? Sharp objects ranging from broken beer bottles to rock and coral outcroppings may be waiting to cut your nylon rope. Steel resists this sort of abuse, which is why sailors cruising near coral reefs often choose all-chain rodes. As will be pointed out in the next chapter, an all-chain rode doesn't always make for a comfortable night in rough water. However, in coral-infested anchorages chain gives a more secure feeling than a nylon rode. Coral chews through nylon, but the worst it will do to chain is grind off the galvanizing.

Table 2-5

CHAIN SIZE	PROOF COIL	HIGH TEST	BBB	GALVANIZED SHACKLE
3/16"	750			
1/4"	1,250	2,500		1,000
5/16"	1,875	4,000	1,950	1,500
3/8"	2,625	5,100	2,750	2,000
1/2"	4,500	8,200		4,000

Note: Consult manufacturer of chain for exact breaking-strength data.

Double-galvanized proof-coil chain is a staple item on American farms. The best prices for it are usually found in stores catering to farmers. These stores buy full coils and cut sections to length. Farm stores also carry a selection of galvanized screw-pin shackles at more attractive prices than marine stores. Be sure that both the chain and the shackles have a heavy coat of rust-preventing zinc galvanizing, especially for saltwater service. Also be sure the breaking strengths are equal to the intended purpose.

Plastic-Coated Chain

Boat stores offer short lengths of plastic-coated chain that claim to be less likely to damage fiberglass gel coats. Unfortunately, most of these coated chains are too short to provide enough weight to be of any real value. Few are longer than four feet. Also, the plastic coating makes the chain stiff, so that it tends to accentuate unfair pull by the rode on the anchor shank.

Acco, a major U.S. chain manufacturer, produces a polymer-coated version of standard proof-coil chain. Each link in this chain is free of its neighbors, yet is fully coated with white plastic. The coating provides some protection for decks without reducing the flexibility of the chain. Acco coated chain is available in two sizes: ¼ inch by 5 feet and ⁵⁄₁₆ inch by 6 feet. Large connecting links on both ends make it easy to install shackles.

Galvanized Shackles

Galvanized screw-pin or loose-pin shackles are used to attach the chain to both the anchor and the eye splice in the nylon rope. Avoid using undersized shackles. The shackle pin must be at least equal in diameter to the thickness of the chain. Some authorities call for pins 30 percent thicker than the chain. A seizing of stainless steel or Monel Metal wire must *always* be used to keep screw pins from unscrewing at inoppor-

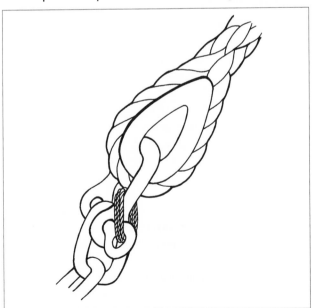

Screw-pin shackles used in ground tackle should be seized (or "moused") with stainless steel wire to prevent them from accidentally coming loose.

tune moments. Loose pins should be retained with conventional bent cotter pins and not the more convenient cotter rings. These pins require regular inspection for corrosion or wear.

Seizing wire can be found at sailboat chandlers or in catalogs catering to sailors. It comes on a large spool with enough wire to last a dozen lifetimes. Most stores sell shorter lengths at a substantial markup. Although the cost per foot is higher, a three- or four-foot length is the most economical way to purchase enough wire to seize a dozen or so shackles.

Tubular Connectors

A traditional shackle may be too large to fit through the anchor roller housing. Special tubular connectors are sold to solve this problem. They are roughly the same diameter as a link of chain, with one end designed to attach to the anchor while the other connects to the chain. Tubular anchor connectors are excellent for lunch hooks or working anchors that are not used for extended mooring. They are not suggested on storm anchors or on permanent moorings that are left in the water for extended periods of time.

Rope-to-Chain Splices

A rope-to-chain splice avoids the bulk of a shackle or the potential weakness of a tubular connector. This type of splice is required by some electric windlasses equipped with combination wildcat/gypsies. Without a splice, you must switch the rode manually from the wildcat to the gypsy.

A rope-to-chain splice is little more than an eye splice with an eye only large enough to fit through one link of chain. With three-strand twisted rope, two strands are passed through the link one way and the third comes through in the opposite direction. The splice is then finished in the conventional manner with the appropriate number of tucks (minimum of three

for manila; four or more for nylon) plus an extra round of tucks for security.

Chain Swivels

Boats that never anchor longer than a couple of hours have few problems with twisted anchor chain. If mooring lasts several days, however, the normal swinging of the boat around the anchor will twist hockles into the chain. Enough force can be generated in these hockles to break the chain. This situation is prevented by inserting a swivel between the chain and the anchor to accommodate the boat's movements.

Wire Anchor Rode

All-wire anchor rodes are seldom seen aboard pleasure boats. They are difficult to handle with the winches or windlasses available from the average chandlery. Wire rope cannot be fed into a rope locker for storage. It must be wound onto the reel of a drum-type winch. The available equipment is large, cumbersome, and not suited for the small confines of a yacht.

However, including a section of wire rope between the chain and the anchor may increase holding power. Tests show that a wire attached to the anchor allows it to penetrate deeper into the bottom than if it had chain attached. Up to a 25 percent increase in the holding power of the anchor has been reported in soft bottoms such as loose sand, gravel, or loose clay.

The section of wire rope should be at least three feet long, although it can be equal in length to the chain that follows. Chain is still needed because it weighs about eight times as much as wire of equivalent breaking strength. The chain section of the rode does not bury, but remains on top of the seabed where it performs its traditional function of keeping the pull on the anchor as horizontal as possible.

Wire rope chosen for this purpose should be

either stainless steel or heavily galvanized mild steel to prevent corrosion. The greater the number of individual wires in the rope, the greater its flexibility. Wire rope of 6 x 24 construction (6 strands of 24 wires each) has enough flex to bend through deck fittings.

DECK GEAR

Misguided "stylists" who design modern powerboats perceive the foredeck as a seagoing automobile hood. They transform what should be a working deck into a gleaming expanse unbroken by "ugly" (in their lubberly eyes) protrusions such as anchoring or mooring cleats. Or these stylists compromise by allowing installation of only the smallest possible hardware. As a result, the majority of U.S. production boats lack proper deck gear such as cleats, bitts, and chocks for anchoring.

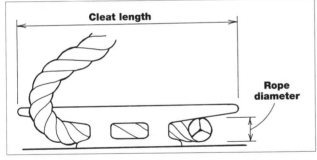

Large, well-placed deck cleats are the mark of a thoughtful boat builder. Too often, factory-installed cleats are inadequate for serious anchoring or mooring. There is a relationship between the diameter of the rope and the correct size cleat. As a rule, cleats should be 2 inches in overall length for every ⅛ inch of rope diameter.

Cleat Size and Installation

Experience has shown a direct relationship between the overall length of a cleat and the diameter of rope that it can safely accommo-

date. The rule of thumb is that cleats should be 2 inches in overall length for every ⅛ inch of rope diameter. This formula produces Table 2-6.

Repairing boat factory omissions requires installing adequate cleats or a center mooring bitt on the foredeck. New hardware must be through-bolted and have metal backing plates to spread

Table 2-6

Suggested Cleat Size	
ROPE DIAMETER	CLEAT LENGTH
1/4"	4"
3/8"	6"
1/2"	8"
5/8"	10"
3/4"	12"
1"	16"

loads over as wide an area of deck as possible. Many fiberglass boats have sandwich deck construction with balsa or other core materials between the layers of glass. If this is the case, it may be best to let a professional do the installation to avoid delamination or weakening of the deck structure.

Rollers and Platforms

A twelve- to fifteen-pound anchor and fifteen feet of chain are about all the weight a healthy male can hoist off the bottom using only his strong arms. Such lightweight ground tackle is suitable only for smaller runabouts or daysailers. Serious anchoring of cruising boats requires ground tackle too heavy for comfortable use of "Swedish steam" (muscle power). Well-designed anchor rollers are the least expensive way of reducing the back-breaking work of hoisting anchor. They allow the use of heavier ground tackle, which increases the safety of the vessel.

A roller allows the rode to be *pulled* aboard

This well-engineered bow platform is molded into the hull of the boat. It is equipped with an oversize roller designed for a Bruce anchor. Sacrificial plastic pieces defend the fiberglass against damage from the anchor flukes.

using the muscles of the back and legs as well as those of the arms. Without a roller, the anchor and rode must be *lifted* over the gunwale using arm muscles alone. Anchors up to thirty-five pounds can be safely raised with the help of a roller. Larger anchors still require mechanical winches or windlasses.

Install the largest practical diameter anchor roller. The larger the roller wheel, the easier it is to haul in the rode. A 2½-inch-diameter roller is the absolute minimum acceptable size. It should be grooved (scored) to accept the rope. High-quality rollers are made of synthetic rubber or long-wearing plastic materials. Smooth operation is ensured by an axle pin that is a minimum ⅜ inch in diameter. The pin should be easily removable to facilitate changing a worn or damaged rubber roller. Everything should be contained by a stainless steel framework that is bolted to the boat.

Special roller assemblies are designed to match the individual configurations of CQR, Bruce, and other plow-style or stock-in-head Danforth anchors. A properly matched assembly

forces the anchor to rotate into its correct stowage position as it comes through the roller. Once the anchor is stowed, a captive pin secures it for sea. Anchors and roller assemblies should be purchased as matched sets. A roller assembly for a CQR won't work properly with a Danforth or a Bruce anchor.

A well-built bow platform is the best place for mounting an anchor roller. Position the roller so that the anchor stows in the roller on the platform. This stowage is convenient with Danforth-style anchors, but is absolutely necessary with plow-style anchors. Platform stowage avoids moving a cumbersome lump of cast metal around on deck. Also, lowering a platform-mounted anchor involves little more than letting it roll off the bow. When hoisting, the roller guides the chain and shackles aboard and rolls the anchor into its proper position for storage.

Anchor platforms must be strongly braced. Not only do they support the dead weight of the stowed anchor, but they also must withstand live loads from the anchor rode. A sideways pull of the rode can be enough to twist a poorly mounted platform right off the bow. These strains should be taken into account during construction of factory-installed platforms. Don't count on it, however. Some factory bow platforms are little more than cosmetic appendages that need strengthening before serious anchoring can be undertaken.

Platforms can be added to most boats by adapting one of the teak versions offered by aftermarket suppliers. A good teak platform is a minimum of 12 inches wide and made of wood strips at least 1½ inches thick. The strips should be bolted *and* glued together for strength, and the completed platform must be attached to the deck with ⅜-inch or larger stainless steel carriage bolts. Typically, five mounting bolts are used, all with metal backing plates and either lock washers or self-locking nuts. Ideally, bolts are arranged in the same pattern as the pips on the "5" side of a pair of dice.

The roller assembly for a one-anchor setup is set into a slot on the centerline of the platform. This allows the rode to go directly over the stem. The roller assembly is inserted from the top of the platform. Wide flanges prevent it from passing through the platform opening and allow for mounting hardware. With plow-style anchors it may be better to use one of the specialized roller assemblies that installs on top of the platform.

A captive pin in the roller assembly prevents the anchor from slipping overboard, but it will not prevent rattling while under way. Windline Marine's AT-3 anchor tensioner is designed to take up the slack on anchors up to ninety pounds. It's just a simple hook attached to a stainless steel latching mechanism. The hook grabs the chain, which is pulled tight by closing the latch. Once the chain's tight, there should be no more rattles.

Winches and Windlasses

Hauling up an anchor is hard. Expect the "anchor yanker" to work up a sweat, especially when trying to break out an anchor that's firmly dug into the bottom. If there's a teenage football player aboard, no problem. But not every boat has such a handy crew member. The solution is a mechanical winch or windlasses to do the heavy hauling. In modern nautical parlance, a *winch* has a vertically mounted drum, while a *windlass* drum is horizontal. These terms are occasionally confused by everyone, including the equipment manufacturers themselves.

A manual anchor winch is almost identical to its cousins used on sailboats to handle sheets and halyards. Incoming anchor rope wraps around the vertical drum. A standard winch handle inserted into the top of the drum provides

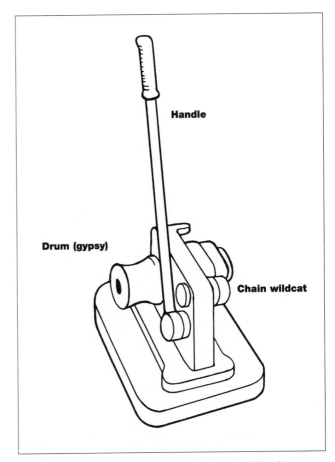

A manual anchor windlass eases the burden of raising heavy ground tackle. This one has a rope drum and a separate chain wildcat. The handle is removed when not in use.

motive power. Initial mechanical advantage comes from the size difference between the diameter of the drum and the length of the winch handle. Optional mechanical gearing inside the winch body may provide additional power. A typical manual anchor winch has a 5:1 mechanical advantage, meaning one pound of force on the handle yields nearly five pounds of pull on the rode. (There is always some power loss to friction.) Some winches also have a chain wildcat located below the rope drum.

Both Simpson Lawrence and Maxwell produce electrically powered vertical anchor winches. These units take up less deck space than horizontal-drum windlasses, an important factor on smaller craft. Tension must be kept on the line coming off the drum or no force will be exerted on the rode. This tension is provided manually in a process called *tailing*. Tailed-off

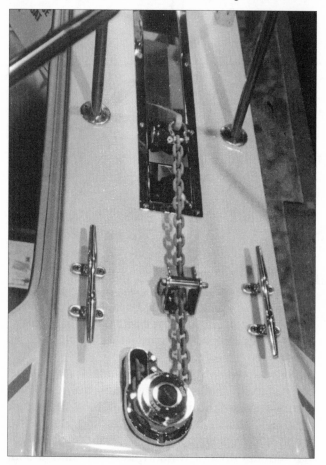

This vertical winch serves the anchor platform seen on page 36. It has a combined rope/chain wildcat. Power comes from an electric motor or a hand crank. A chain stopper takes the weight of the anchor off the winch when the anchor is stowed.

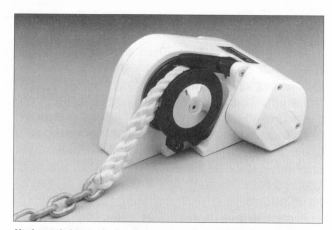

Horizontal-drum windlasses are easy to install because all of the working parts are above deck. This unit has a combined rope/chain wildcat. Note the neat rope-to-chain splice. *(Courtesy Simpson Lawrence)*

rope piles up on deck until after the anchor is hoisted. Then, once it is dry, the rope is fed down the deck pipe into its locker.

Horizontal-drum windlasses all but eliminate the need for crew on the foredeck to handle the anchor. Remote-control electric units hold the anchor stowed in position on the pulpit, lower it to the bottom, and then raise it back up again. Electric windlasses produced under the Good brand and by Powerwinch allow complete push-button control of the anchor from the helm. Such convenience is costly, but it may be necessary for anyone with health problems or a heart condition. Sedentary sailors in their late forties or early fifties are often advised to avoid the muscle strain of hoisting anchor.

Windlasses that wind conventional rope onto a drum like a fishing reel are fine for lightweight fishing boats, but may create problems on larger vessels. The strain of the rode against the windlass may cause the rope to jam into the turns already on the drum. The result can be an unsuspected tangle. Next time the anchor is dropped, only a short length of the rode pays out before the tangle jams the mechanism. This proscription does not apply to special reels that use flat nylon webbing as the anchor rode. Flat webbing is used because it will not jam on the reel.

The key to push-button anchoring is a windlass with a combination rope drum (or gypsy) and chain wildcat on the same axle. This allows the entire rode—rope and chain—to be hoisted and deposited in the rope locker without shifting from the drum to wildcat by hand. Conventional electric-powered units have separate rope drums and chain wildcats. The drum hauls the rope section of the rode aboard. Then the rode is moved to the wildcat, which hauls in the chain and brings home the anchor on the roller. Most windlasses also have a brake that allows you to control paying out of anchor rode when lowering the anchor.

Whether electric or manual, a winch or windlass should never bear the pull of the rode once the anchor has dug into the bottom. Shock loads and strain can damage expensive gears or brake mechanisms. Such damage is likely to allow the rode to run out, bitter end and all. Belay the rode on a mooring cleat or riding bitt once the anchor is well set on the bottom.

Chain Wildcats

Friction between the relatively smooth drum and fiber rope is sufficient to generate considerable pull on the rode. Chain, however, provides almost no friction against a smooth metal drum. A rope drum just spins inside chain wraps, causing damage to its metal surface. Handling chain takes a special cogged wheel known as a *wildcat*. Slots in the wildcat engage individual links of chain and transfer rotary motion of the wheel into horizontal pull on the rode. The size, shape, and spacing of the cogs varies, depending upon the size and type of chain being used. A wildcat

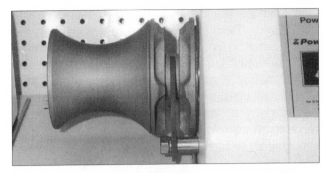

A chain wildcat has special cogs designed to mesh with the links of the anchor chain. This one is located inside a rope gypsy (horizontal winch). Wildcats must be sized to match the chain.

designed for BBB chain will not work correctly with proof-coil or high-test chain.

A word of warning: Don't assume that the wildcat on a foreign-built winch will accept U.S. proof-coil chain. European winches are often made to use "ISO short link" chain, which has links slightly different from chains commonly sold in North America. Or, the unit may be designed for use with BBB chain, which is incompatible with both U.S. proof-coil or ISO short-link chain. Check and *double-check* that the winch will handle the chain. If in doubt, send a twelve- to fifteen-link section of chain to the windlass supplier for matching to the correct wildcat.

Installing a Winch or Windlass

While there are physical differences between winches and windlasses, installation is identical. Both are mounted on the deck near the stem so that the wildcat is aligned with the chock or anchor roller. This alignment is critical to avoid binding or excessive friction on the chain portion of the rode. Achieving the proper alignment may force the winch to be installed off center on the deck. This is caused by the wildcat being located on one side of the mechanism.

A full-size mounting template is included with most units. Tape this template to the deck in the exact location where the winch will be located. Set the winch on top of the template just to be sure anchor rode alignment is correct. Once you're satisfied, set the winch aside and mark the centers of the various holes that must be drilled through the deck. A pencil point pricked through the paper will mark fiberglass. On a wooden deck, prick through the template with an awl to dimple the wood beneath.

Hardware mounting holes should be the same size as the bolts that will hold the winch in place. Mounting hardware is typically ³/₈-inch stainless steel carriage bolts. Drill a hole for the wiring as specified by the winch manufacturer. The largest hole is to send the rode down into the rope locker. Drill bits can be used for holes up to ¹/₂-inch diameter. Larger holes require a hole saw and a powerful electric drill motor.

Polysulfide caulk should be used to seal bolt holes. Polyurethane adhesive/sealants or silicone compounds are not recommended. Oversize fender washers (2-inch diameter or larger) are needed on the underside of the deck to spread the strain of the bolts. If large enough fender washers cannot be found, make your own from ³/₈-inch marine plywood. Standard metal washers will prevent the nuts from crushing the wood. Conventional lock washers or self-locking aircraft nuts must be used to prevent vibration from loosening the nuts.

Electric winches must be wired *directly* to the boat's main battery. Connection should never be made to the regular distribution bus because winches gobble enormous amounts of electricity. Ordinary distribution wiring is not adequate for the job. At a minimum, wires from the battery to the winch should be AWG #8 on runs of less than thirty feet and AWG #6 on longer runs. Heavy-gauge wires keep voltage drop to a minimum.

Even a small drop in voltage severely reduces the power of the winch. Large wires are also less likely to overheat under load and cause an electrical fire.

Special circuit breakers are supplied with electric winches. These breakers *must* be used for protection. Install the breaker at the battery positive (+) terminal connection of the winch wiring. Use a crimp-on ring connector to attach the feed wire to the breaker. If the boat is equipped with a battery selector switch, the breaker can be installed on the output stud of this switch. The negative (-) ground wire from the winch should go directly to the appropriate battery terminal. Run both wires in a direct path to the winch, being sure to keep them high out of the bilge. Nonmetallic wiring supports should be used every eighteen inches.

Windlasses that require manual tailing of the incoming anchor line need a foot switch on the foredeck. This allows one person to simultaneously control the winch motor and tail the rode. A foot switch should be located conveniently near the windlass, but out of the normal traffic pattern. Look for a location where the person tailing the incoming line can also operate the switch. Drill an appropriate hole in the deck for the switch and mount it with self-tapping screws using the gasket supplied. If this switch controls main power to the winch, it should be wired into the positive (+) red wire from the battery.

Low-voltage control wiring is necessary for remotely operated winches. The heavy power circuit is the same as described above, except that the foot switch is eliminated. Control wires generally come as a wiring harness supplied by the manufacturer. One end plugs into the winch while the other goes to a panel mounted on the control console.

Choose the position for the remote control panel with care. Avoid locations where it might be accidentally bumped while you are under way. This could result in the anchor being dropped unexpectedly. (Consider the carnage that would result if a propeller got wrapped by the anchor rode at 30 knots.) Use the template supplied by the manufacturer to drill the appropriate mounting holes.

Chafe Protection

Chafe occurs whenever a rope is bent or pulled over a sharp edge. *Sharp* is a relative word. An edge doesn't have to be the keenness of a barber's razor if the bend of the rope is sufficiently acute. The best protection against chafe is to lead the rode in as straight a line as possible from the mooring bitt all the way down to the anchor. If that can't be done, special efforts should be taken to reduce the sharpness of angles and bends.

Chafe is always a consideration when picking appropriate deck hardware such as cleats or bitts. Sharp edges or rough surfaces from poor casting techniques can quickly wear out the nylon rope. The best cleats and mooring bitts are softly rounded with no sharp corners. The worst offenders in terms of sharp edges are chromed bronze mooring posts being imported from the Far East. While these foreign-made mooring posts are quite attractive, their sharp square edges are murder on rope.

Boats with teak toe rails often have stainless steel antiwear strips protecting the wood. The purpose of these strips is to prevent ropes from abrading the varnish or wearing grooves in the teak. Their function is not to protect the ropes. In fact, burrs in the slots of the screws holding the strips in place can quickly chafe synthetic rope.

Bow Chocks

A cast bronze or stainless steel chock protects the boat and its anchor rode from each other.

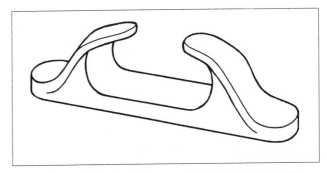

Chocks are designed to keep the rope in place and protect it against chafe. Undersize chocks are often installed on production boats. Replace them according to Table 2-7.

The chock also keeps the rode properly aligned over the bow. Without a chock, the anchor rope jumps around on the foredeck, increasing the tendency of the boat to yaw around its anchor. As important as they are, chocks are seen on fewer and fewer new powerboats these days. Equally troublesome, the chocks that do appear are usually woefully undersize. Since designs vary, it is difficult to relate the size of a chock to a specific diameter rope. Table 2-7 gives approximate guidelines.

Table 2-7

Chock Size (approximate)	
OVERALL LENGTH	ROPE DIAMETER
3"	3/8"
4"	1/2"
5"	5/8"
6"	3/4"

Bow chocks are canted to accommodate the pointed shape of the boat near the front end. They are often sold as "pairs" of port and starboard, but in truth rotating any canted chock 180 degrees changes it from port to starboard duty. Stern chocks are straight since the transom is normally straight across the width of the boat. *Skene pattern chocks* have longer horns that may end in enlarged bulbs. Longer horns hold the rope securely in the chock even if the boat is dancing wildly in rough water.

Windline Marine offers a stainless steel locking chock with a captive threaded bolt designed to hold rope up to one inch in diameter. Once the bolt is closed, the chock effectively becomes a closed fairlead with no opening for the rope to jump out of. All metal edges are carefully rounded. (Closed chocks are sometimes called *Panama chocks* on large ships, since they are required of vessels transiting the Panama Canal.)

A roller is one of the best means of preventing chafe of the anchor rode. As the boat moves around the anchor, the rope rolls on the wheel. Rolling reduces friction as much as possible. A large-diameter wheel also lessens wear by reducing the sharp bend where the rode leaves the boat. The majority of anchor rollers hold the rope captive to ensure that the rode is always pulling on the centerline of the boat.

Another interesting product from Windline is its stern fairlead anchor roller. This assembly is V-shaped so that any sideways movement of the rope brings it into contact with a roller. It is designed for use on the stern, although there's no reason it could not be used elsewhere on the boat. A pivoting bail held by a thumbscrew prevents the rope from jumping out of this chock.

Chafing Gear

Chafe can also be prevented by wrapping the line with cloth or leather. Materials used in this manner are collectively known as *chafing gear*. Rags are okay in an emergency, but are otherwise not much good for preventing chafe. Cotton (the typical fiber of rags) doesn't have much chafe resistance of its own, so cotton rags wear out rapidly.

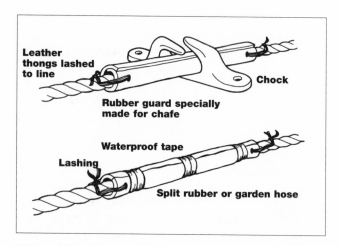

Rubber chafing gear can be purchased, or similar equipment can be homemade from a piece of rubber hose.

Also, keeping a wad of rags in place around the rope is a problem that almost defies solution.

Leather strips can be sewn onto ropes at spots where chafe is expected. This solution works on dock lines where chafe always occurs at the same spot, but is impossible with an anchor rode. The same amount of anchor line is not let out each time the boat is anchored. Sewing a leather antichafe strip onto the rode for every anchoring is not a likely possibility. So leather strips aren't the answer for protecting an anchor rode any more than rags.

Short lengths of pliable water hose can be slit lengthwise to allow them to snap over the rode. This type of chafing gear is available commercially, but can be made at home at almost no cost. The inside diameter of the hose should be slightly larger than the diameter of the rope it is to protect. Cut a section between eighteen and twenty-four inches long and slit it from end to end. The slit can be straight or you can let it spiral slightly around the hose. Drill a quarter-inch hole in the hose wall at either end for lashing cords made of leather thongs.

Antichafe hoses are snapped over the rope where it goes through the chock or over a sharp bend. Lashings are wrapped several times around the rope, then tied tightly to prevent the hose from moving. All of the chafe is now focused on the outside of the hose and not on the rope. Hoses used this way have a drawback. They may have an outside diameter too large for the boat's chocks. Being oversize, they may jump out of chocks at inopportune moments.

ANCHOR STOWAGE

Large sailing ships were built with special timbers called *cat heads* to hold their huge stock anchors. Later, early power yachts were equipped with anchor cranes to handle their Herreshoff pattern anchors. Neither piece of equipment is installed aboard power- or sailboats today, but the problem of stowing the anchor remains.

Small Boat Stowage

A perfect solution to the problem of stowing both the anchor and its attached rode aboard small boats will never be found. Space for coils or rope and heavy ground tackle is notoriously lacking on vessels under eighteen feet in length. The tendency is to throw everything in the bottom of the boat, where it is slowly trampled into a tangled mess. This leads to frustrating moments when the time comes to drop the hook.

The primary goals of anchor stowage are to keep ground tackle from underfoot, and to keep it orderly and ready for instant deployment. Placing the rope, chain, and anchor into a common container has proven the most effective way of accomplishing these goals. Two inexpensive containers are a canvas anchor bag and a flexible plastic laundry basket.

ANCHOR BAG

This is basically a reinforced canvas satchel large enough to hold the anchor and rode. A grommet in the bottom allows the bitter end to be secured to the boat before the anchor is lowered. Synthetic canvas (e.g., Acrilan) is suggested, as dampness associated with anchors will rot cotton fabrics.

LAUNDRY BASKETS

Flexible plastic baskets, which come in a variety of sizes and styles, can be jammed into odd corners of the boat. Coil the anchor line into the basket and lay the anchor on top. It may be necessary to cut a small opening in the side near the bottom for access to the bitter end.

Anchor rope is normally coiled and secured with a sea gasket for stowage in an anchor bag. A basket is easier to use because the rope doesn't need to be neatly coiled. Just let wet bights of line fall into the basket as the anchor is raised. Rope can be piled randomly into a basket without fear of tangles as long as it remains untouched during storage. The open mesh of the basket allows air circulation to dry the line.

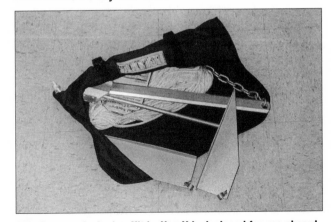

The Commando Anchor Kit by Nav-X is designed for use aboard inflatable boats and other small craft. It contains a disassembled anchor, chain, and rope for boats up to sixteen feet in length.

The Nav-X company produces something called a Commando Anchor Kit, consisting of a special storage bag, anchor, and line. Designed for boats up to 16 feet, the kit includes a Guardian G-5 aluminum anchor that can be taken apart without tools. This is connected to a 150-foot rode of three-strand 1/4-inch rope. Rolled into a red bag, the whole kit weighs less than eight pounds.

West Marine, the national chain of boat stores, offers a storage bag designed to carry only the rode. Its wide mouth is held open by an internal stainless steel ring for easy deployment. During storage, the bag is closed with a drawstring. A leather-reinforced slit permits the bitter end to be secured outside the bag. This bag isn't big enough to hold an anchor.

Large Boat Stowage

Boats over twenty-six feet in length require anchors far too heavy to be classified as "portable." Bags and such aren't practical. Bow rollers and on-deck storage become the only realistic solutions. This type of stowage requires a rope locker to keep the rode out from under-

Deck pipes come in two styles. The one on the right is a loose cap pipe suitable for larger boats with heavy ground tackle. The pipe on the left has a hinged cap, which is kept closed by a spring.

foot. Introducing a rope locker into the bow of the boat brings the need for a deck pipe (sometimes mistakenly called a "hawse pipe") through which the rode can be sent below.

Two styles of deck pipes are available, one with a hinged cap and the other with a loose cap. The best of both types are made of heavily chromed ("triple plated") brass or bronze. Some loose-cap models are also manufactured out of stainless steel. Bright-finish bronze fittings are available for use on traditional craft.

It's difficult to lose a hinged cap because it's attached to the deck pipe base. This advantage is offset by a smaller-size pipe opening. Hinged-cap fixtures are generally limited to rope one inch or smaller in diameter. They are not large enough to pass an eye splice, so the chain section of the rode must stay on deck. Also, the cap may break at the hinge, requiring replacement of the complete unit.

Loose-cap deck pipes are made in diameters large enough to accommodate both an eye splice and a shackle. Most are oval in shape to allow the chain portion of the rode to be sent below still shackled to the rope. The obvious disadvantage of a loose cap is the possibility of its being kicked overboard. Manufacturers use light beaded "keeper" chains (or heavy monofilament line) to prevent this accident, but these keepers seldom last more than a couple of seasons. After that, retaining the cap aboard depends upon the diligence of the foredeck crew.

It's impossible to make either style deck pipe completely watertight because chain or rope exits through them at all times. The cap is intended only to keep green water out of the boat when the bow goes seas under. Because seawater always penetrates, a deck pipe should never lead into V-berths or other areas where bedding or clothing might be soaked.

The rope locker should be located directly beneath the deck pipe. This lets gravity help tumble the rode below. An offset deck pipe requires someone to crawl forward and pull the rope down into the locker. It's a messy, seasick-prone job that's best avoided. Good design allows a single person working on deck to both haul the anchor aboard and send the rode down into its locker.

Let the rope pile up in large bights inside the locker. As long as they remain undisturbed, the rode will pay out smoothly the next time the boat comes to anchor. Coiling the line in the rope locker is not recommended because each loop of the coil puts a half twist into the rope. These half twists sometimes cause the rope to tangle as it comes out of the deck pipe. Also, twists put torque into the rope, which may cause twisting force to be applied to the anchor. This can cause the anchor to break out of the bottom.

Two rodes should never be stowed in the same rope locker. To do so invites a massive tangle. Large lockers can be divided in half with a bulkhead. Each half of the divided locker must be served with its own deck pipe. For fiber rodes, make the bulkhead out of minimum $3/8$-inch marine plywood properly sealed and painted. Locker dividers for all-chain rodes must be specially strengthened to accept the weight of the metal links.

Rope lockers are always damp. Water comes aboard in the fibers of the rope as well as down the opening in the deck pipe. Dampness, of course, is the prime contributor to mildew. Nylon rope is not harmed by mildew (other than appearance), but the same can't be said of clothing, bedding, or interior furnishings. Mildew infestations of a boat's living accommodations are often traced to moisture from a wet anchor rode in the rope locker.

Several things can be done to prevent this:

Locker Drain
Puddled water in the bottom of the rope locker should be drained overboard via a through-hull fitting. If this is not feasible, drain the water into the bilge, where it can be pumped overboard.

Ventilation
Moving air is the best way to both dry the rope and prevent mildew. A small ventilator set in the foredeck usually does the job. Remove the cowl and seal the opening with a deck plate when under way, especially in foul weather. Internal ventilation from other compartments of a fiberglass boat is not recommended as it increases the possibility of mildew in the living accommodations. Free flow of air through all compartments of a wooden boat should never be obstructed.

Hatch Gasket
Rope locker openings that go directly into V-berth areas of fiberglass boats should have foam rubber gaskets to block movement of water vapor and mildew spores. Self-stick weather stripping available at any hardware store works well.

Good housekeeping is the best way to prevent mildew. Whenever possible the rode should be allowed to drain on deck before being sent below. Inspect the rope locker regularly for mildew. If telltale black specks are found, wash down the locker with a mild solution of household bleach in water to kill the mildew spores. Drain holes should be probed with a stiff wire to be sure they are not clogged.

General Considerations
Weight is a major factor in anchor stowage,

especially on a sailboat, where weight in the bow reduces performance. That's why hard-core racing sailors store their anchors low in the boat and as close to midships as possible. Such unhandy stowage is permissible on the race course, where anchoring is seldom necessary. Cruising sailors, on the other hand, need to keep their anchors continuously available. They are willing to trade a slight decrease in sailing performance for easier anchoring.

Few powerboat owners are aware of the effects of weight placed far forward on their boats. High-speed powerboats with their narrow hulls particularly suffer from carrying too much weight forward, where it increases the severity of pitching or "porpoising."

Despite the problems associated with weight forward, the only convenient location for a plow-style anchor is on an appropriate bow roller. CQR or Bruce anchors are too bulky to be carried around on deck or stowed in cockpit lockers. This limits the use of plow-style anchors to boats that can carry weight far forward without objectionable loss of performance. It also prevents using them on boats where the installation of a roller assembly is impractical or undesirable. Such cases require the use of lightweight patent anchors such as a Danforth or a Fortress.

The dominance of Danforth and similar-design anchors on U.S. boats has led to the development of dozens of storage gimcracks. While the number of brackets, hangers, and chocks seems bewildering, there are really only two broad categories: rail hangers and deck chocks. Rail hangers allow the anchor to be hung off bow pulpits or lifeline stanchions. Deck chocks prevent the anchor from moving when it is stowed flat on deck.

Sail- and powerboats with stainless steel bow pulpits find rail mounting to be most effective. A single anchor is normally hung in the center of the bow. If two bowers are carried, they are set to port and starboard. Check the size of the pulpit tubing before ordering a bracket. The stainless steel tubing used for bow rails and pulpits has either a 7/8-inch or a 1-inch outside diameter. Most (but not all) anchor brackets will fit either size.

Bronze deck chocks are available to hold Danforth or yachtsman anchors flat on the deck. Powerboats during the wooden-boat era sported their anchors prominently on their foredecks. Anchors were painted to match the vessel. Well-worn paint proudly attested to the owner's successful vacation cruise. Such a display is colorful, but not always practical. More toes have been stubbed on deck-mounted anchors than on any other piece of boating equipment. And the round stock of a Danforth seems to reach out to grab dock lines and sailboat sheets.

Anchor Lockers

A couple of decades ago sailboats started incorporating shallow wells in their foredecks to hold an anchor. A hinged hatch served to keep anchor and rode out of sight, yet easily accessible. Anchor lockers quickly became the standard method of stowage on sailboats over twenty feet. It wasn't long before powerboat designers took the hint and began incorporating similar lockers in their vessels.

The main advantage of an anchor locker is stowage that's quick and easy. When the cover is closed, the anchor is hidden from view. Nobody can see whether the rode was coiled neatly or just jammed into the locker. On the negative side, the large hatch can be cumbersome to open, especially in foul weather. A few characteristics of a good anchor locker are:

A foredeck anchor locker provides convenient storage for the anchor rode. Some are also designed to house the anchor. Note the notch in the forward hatch coaming to allow the anchor rode to run out of the locker with the hatch shut.

• Positive Latch—Needed to keep the locker cover closed even during severe pitching or rolling conditions. This prevents the anchor from accidentally being deployed by a large wave.

• Strong Hinges—A large hatch such as used on an anchor locker can exert considerable strain on its hinges, which consequently must be overbuilt.

• Structurally Sound Cover—An anchor locker is always underfoot when docking or handling sails on the bow. The cover must be strong enough to support the weight of a large adult.

• Oversize Drain—The cover is not watertight, so provision must be made to drain water that enters around the edges. Oversized drains are recommended because these lockers often collect dead leaves or other debris that clogs small openings.

It's a good idea to install a set of deck chocks inside an anchor locker to prevent the anchor from bouncing around while you are under way.

3

ANCHORING BASICS

Anchoring is the process of keeping a boat in one spot by hooking it to the bottom. Modern anchors easily penetrate sand, pebbles, or other soft material, so getting hooked appears easy until the problem is studied in detail. Real-world conditions are seldom as perfect as manufacturers' sales literature. Successful anchoring is as much art as it is science. Your experience as a skipper is a bigger factor in your success than any particular brand or style of anchor. And even so-called experts learn something new every time they drop the hook.

Anchor manufacturers demonstrate miniature versions of their products at boat shows by dragging a tiny anchor across a box full of sand. The idea is to let people see how quickly their brand digs into the bottom. However, a real anchorage isn't a box of sand under bright lights. You can't see what's happening down on the real bottom from the foredeck of a boat. Setting a real anchor is always done "blind," with no way of knowing how well the anchor is digging into the bottom. What's happening on the bottom is a minor mystery that becomes an enigma if the anchor doesn't hold.

Practice is the only way to learn the art of anchoring. Devoting special sessions to learning the basics is the best way to get the required practice. Start with simple situations like setting a lunch hook. Drop the anchor, set it, and veer out the proper rode. Then retrieve the anchor and go through the whole drill again. Due to the physical exertion involved in weighing anchor, two or three practice anchorings are plenty for one session. After that, everyone will be tired and practicing won't be fun anymore.

A "simple situation" involves setting a single anchor in calm water with moderate winds and current. These are the ideal conditions for practice sessions. Learning to set a single hook teaches all of the basic steps of anchoring. Later, when you have mastered the basics, you can add such complexities as a second anchor.

CHOOSING THE ANCHORAGE

Choosing the right spot to drop the hook is the first step in successful anchoring. The three most important criteria are: shelter from the weather; good holding conditions on the bottom; and water depth.

Shelter from Weather

This involves two components. One is protection from wind, the other from waves. Some anchorages offer one but not the other. Protection from waves is normally the more important consideration.

The only thing constant about the weather is change. An anchorage perfectly protected from east winds may be vulnerable to south or west

The first step in successful anchoring is choosing the right place to drop the hook. These boats are moored in a sheltered Maine cove.

winds. If plans call for spending the night on the hook, your must consider the effect of a wind shift before morning. An overnight anchorage must provide protection from both the original wind direction at dusk and the expected new direction overnight.

Sailors recognize a phenomenon called *wind shadow.* This is an area of relative calm in the lee of tall objects such as trees and buildings. These sometimes provide considerable protection against the wind for a distance offshore. However, getting the benefit from their lee requires anchoring relatively close to shore. This can be a dangerous location if the wind shifts 100 degrees or more. Instead of being protected, your boat is now in danger of being driven ashore.

Holding Conditions

These are determined by the type of bottom. The following types of bottoms are listed in order of desirability for setting an anchor:

Hard Sand—Excellent
Clay—Excellent
Hard Mud—Good
Shells, Gravel—Fair to Good
Gravel, Loose Sand—Poor
Soft Mud, Marl—Very Poor
Rocks—Variable*
Heavy Weeds—Nearly Impossible

*Setting an anchor (particularly a Danforth style) in rocks can be difficult. However, once an anchor becomes wedged between two rocks, it may never come loose.

At one time, government charts displayed more useful information about conditions on the bottom. That was back in the days when depth soundings were actually made with an old-fashioned lead line. The sounding crew would "arm" the lead with tallow to bring up a sample of the bottom. Information about bottom samples would later be noted on the published charts. Today, depths are sometimes charted by infrared aerial surveys and other methods not capable of bringing up bottom samples.

There are several ways to collect bottom information on your own. One of the most enjoyable is to talk to other people who have anchored in an area before. Cruising sailors are glad to share their local knowledge. If you can't locate anyone who has visited a particular spot, you may have to do some bottom surveying before choosing your final anchorage. The time-honored method of arming the lead is still the most dependable way of sampling

Arming the Lead

Lead sounding weights cast in the traditional pattern have a hollow cavity. This cavity is intended to be filled with tallow from the galley. Being both sticky and waterproof, the tallow brings up a sample of whatever is on the bottom. If tallow isn't part of your normal ship's stores, try using any waterproof grease. The lead should be "bounced" on the bottom, then quickly brought back to the surface before any of the captured material has time to wash away.

the bottom. Some modern electronic depth sounders give hints about the bottom. An operator adept at reading their displays can usually distinguish mud or rock from weeds.

Knowing the nature of the bottom is only marginally useful without knowledge of the holding characteristics of your boat's anchors. Here's where a personal record of anchor performance comes in handy. Two different brands of anchor may theoretically have the same holding capacity, but each works best under different conditions. Every time you drop the hook, log the type and size of anchor used. Note the nature of the bottom and the wind and sea conditions. Over

time this log will give you a good indication of which anchor works best under what conditions.

Checking the Chart

Information needed to choose a good anchorage can be obtained from two government publications: a nautical chart and a Coast Pilot book. The chart presents a pictorial view of the anchorage, while the book gives an extensive written description of the area. Information on the chart is not duplicated in the Pilot book. Rather, the book contains the sort of local knowledge that cannot be drawn on a chart. Neither should be used without reference to the other.

Water Depth

The possibility of "drying out" at low tide must be examined in tidal waters. Many otherwise ideal anchorages become mud flats twice a day, thanks to the tides.

Depth information is much more plentiful (and accurate) than details about bottom conditions. As a rule, depths on U.S. charts are charted at *mean lower low water*. This means that if the chart says there is six feet of water in a harbor, that's how much would be expected at all but the lowest of low tides. Keep in mind, however, that unusually low tides may occasionally result in less water than charted. Consulting an official tide table to calculate the predicted depth of water at low tide is always prudent.

Chart Datum

Water depths on charts are given with reference to something called *chart datum*. For U.S. coastal charts, this is usually *mean lower low water*. Most tidal waters have two high and two low tides each day. One high water is always higher than the other. Likewise, one low water is always lower. Only the lowest of the two low tides for each day over an extended period of time was averaged in calculating

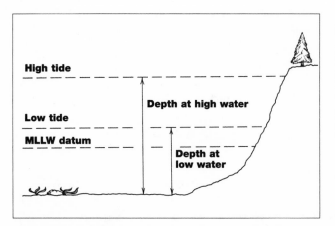

Chart datum for depths on most U.S. coastal areas is *mean lower low water*. This datum was chosen because under normal circumstances there will be more depth available than shown on the chart.

the datum. Using *mean lower low water* minimizes the chance that a low tide will result in less water in the harbor than is shown on the chart.

A *tide table* is needed to calculate the depth of water at any specific time on a given date. These tables are published by the government as well as by private companies. They give the expected height and time of both high and low waters. An additional formula allows calculation of the state of the tide at any time between high and low water.

Heights taken from tide tables are added to the depths printed on the chart. For example, the charted depth of a harbor may be 6 feet, and the height of the tide at low water is given in the tide table as +4 feet. This results in an expected depth of 10 feet in the harbor:

$$
\begin{array}{ll}
6' & \text{Charted depth} \\
+4' & \text{Height of tide} \\
\hline
10' & \text{Expected harbor depth}
\end{array}
$$

Wind and wave action can cause significant variations in the state of the tide from the predictions

in published tide tables, so take note.

Great Lakes sailors do not have to contend with tides, but the water levels of the individual lakes are constantly changing. In any year, the difference between the highest and lowest level may be five feet or more. Swings of two to four feet during a single day are not uncommon during storms. The United States and Canada jointly developed the *International Great Lakes Datum*, from which an individual *low water datum* for each of the five lakes was developed. Charted depths refer to the individual lake low water datum. In order to calculate the exact depth of water it is necessary to know the variation of the specific lake from its datum. This variation is added to (if the lake is high) or subtracted from (if the lake is below datum) the charted depth.

Example: How much water would you expect in Put-in-Bay on Lake Erie if the charted depth is 6 feet and the lake is 2 feet over datum?

$$
\begin{array}{ll}
6' & \text{Charted depth} \\
+2' & \text{Height of lake over datum} \\
\hline
8' & \text{Expected depth}
\end{array}
$$

Information on lake heights above or below datum is broadcast daily by the U.S. Coast Guard and may be carried on NOAA weather radio stations.

Chart Scale

In picking an anchorage, use the chart with the largest scale. Large-scale charts show the most small detail. A harbor chart with a scale of 1:50,000 or larger is best. If you lack one of these, a Coast Chart may prove useful. Smaller-scale general or sailing charts do not show enough detail to be of much help in picking a harbor.

Shallow-water areas on U.S. charts are tinted blue to accentuate shoals and other dangers to navigation. Blue tint does not indicate the same depth from chart to chart. The depth (or more cor-

Table 3-1

U.S. Chart Scales	
Harbor Chart	1: 50,000 OR LARGER
Coast Chart	1: 50,000 TO 1:150,000
General Chart	1: 150,000 TO 1:600,000
Sailing Chart	1: 600,000 OR SMALLER

rectly, shallowness) at which the blue tint starts changes with the intended purpose of the chart. Additionally, some areas may be tinted green. These are areas that are covered with water at high tide, but often dry out at low tide.

Depth contours are indicated by dotted, dashed, or dot-and-dash lines. The typical pattern of the dots and dashes indicates the depth as shown in Table 3-2. While the water within a depth contour may (or may not) be tinted blue, the contour lines themselves are always printed in black.

Table 3-2

Water Depth Contours			
Depth (IN Feet)	Depth (IN Fathoms)	Depth (IN Meters)	Contour Lines
6	1	1	....
12	2	2	.. ..
18	3	3	... ...
24	4	4	....
30	5	5	....
36	6	6	--- --- --- --- --- ---
60	10	10	—.—.—.—.—.—.—

Submarine cables and pipelines cross waterways used by both large and small vessels. These are indicated by special symbols printed in magenta ink on the chart. The symbol for a sub-

marine cable is a wavy line, while pipelines are shown by dots with thin lines for "tails." Cables and pipelines are not usually described in U.S. Coast Pilot books. Signs may be posted onshore

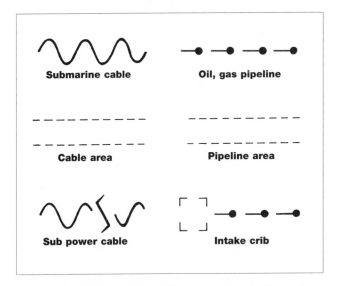

Submarine cables are indicated by a wavy magenta line, submerged pipelines by dots with straight-line "tails." Both are normally printed in magenta ink.

warning mariners of their existence.

Hooking on to a submarine cable can produce serious consequences. Breaking a phone cable deprives innocent people of telephone service. Electric cables carry very high voltage that threatens electrocution of the crew handling the anchor. If the anchor cannot be retrieved without undue strain, the rode should be cut away and left on the bottom. *Never* attempt to cut a submarine cable.

As noted earlier, specific information about the nature of the bottom seems a bit scanty on U.S. charts. However, some valuable data are still noted. Symbols shown in Table 3-3 are normally printed in small black type over the spots where samples of the bottom were taken. For a full listing of all abbreviations, see *NOAA Chart No. 1*.

Table 3-3

Common Symbols for Nature of Seabed		
PRIMARY SYMBOL	**DESCRIPTION**	**ADDITIONAL SYMBOL**
Blds	Boulders	
brk	Broken	bk
Co Hd	Coral Head	
crs	Coarse (sand only)	c
fne	Fine (sand only)	f
Grd	Ground	
Grs	Grass	
hrd	Hard	h
K	Kelp	
m	Medium (sand only)	
Mrl	Marl	
Oys	Oysters	
Oz	Ooze	
sft	Soft	s
Sn	Shingle	
stk	Sticky	sy
stf	Stiff	sf

Charts of tidal waters may also contain arrows indicating the set and drift of currents. An arrow with fletches ("feathers") shows the set (true direction) of a *flood* stream. If the arrow does not have fletches, it shows the set of an *ebb* stream. In both cases, the drift (speed) of the current in knots is shown above the arrow.

DROPPING THE HOOK

All ground tackle should be sorted out and made ready for use before you approach the spot to anchor. Check all shackles to be sure the pins are secure. Pull enough rode out of the rope locker to equal at least twice the depth of water. Fake down the rope so it will pay out smoothly

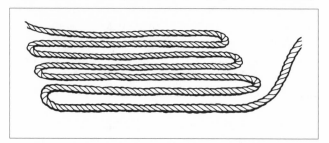

Faking a line involves laying it out in large bights on deck. This allows the rope to pay out without tangles. Faking is also an excellent way to dry a wet anchor rode.

with no hockles or flying turns. *Faking* a line is a method of laying large bights of rope on deck. Each bight is laid next to, but not over top of, its neighbor. Make sure the rode is led through the anchor roller or chock and is not fouled on bitts, lifeline stanchions, or other deck hardware.

Approach Under Power

Determine the speed and direction of both the wind and the current. They are seldom the same, and one will always have a greater effect on your boat than the other. Your final approach should be made heading into the strongest of the two. Wind usually determines the approach of vessels

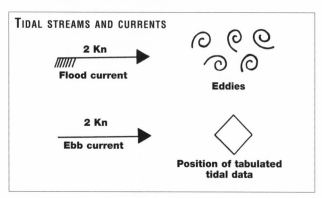

Charts of tidal areas may contain arrows indicating the set and drift of flood and ebb currents. Fletches ("feathers") on the arrow indicate a flood current. If the arrow does not have fletches, it indicates an ebb current. Drifts are in knots.

with large amounts of superstructure or rigging. Deep-draft sailboats may find a subsurface current that forces a crosswind approach. If doubt exists about whether current or wind dominates, make a "dry run" approach to gain knowledge of the prevailing conditions.

The final approach should be made at bare steerageway for the prevailing conditions. Your exact approach speed changes with the weather. Use a slower speed in calm weather, faster in high winds or strong currents. Shift into neutral just before reaching the spot to anchor and allow the boat to lose way as it coasts forward. You should lose all way directly over the spot where the anchor will be dropped. If this doesn't happen, don't be afraid to make another approach. Never drop the hook if the boat is making even slight headway.

The anchor is *lowered* to the bottom just as the boat loses all way. In sailor talk, the lowering is done "smartly" (quickly, yet under total control). On smaller boats under about twenty-four feet this can be done by letting the rode slip through gloved hands. Larger boats with heavier ground tackle require mechanical control of the rode. Taking a round turn on the drum puts the weight and strain of the anchor on the windlass instead of on the human being tending the anchor.

If a windlass isn't available, the rode should be *surged* under one horn of a mooring cleat. Friction of the rope against the cleat keeps the rode under control as the anchor descends to the bottom.

Wind and current will not let the boat stay positioned over the drop spot for more than a few moments. The boat will naturally gather sternway. Two mistakes are common during the few seconds after the anchor hits the bottom:

• Chain Pileup—Chain piling up on top of the anchor can foul the stock, shank, or flukes. If

---

Scope

Scope is defined as the amount of rode between the boat and the anchor. This includes the dry rope from the waterline up to the deck. Rode can be expressed either in linear measurement (feet, yards, fathoms, etc.) or as a ratio based on the depth of the water. The accepted rule of thumb holds that scope should be five to seven times the depth of water. This rule works for the majority of situations, but scope must be increased in foul weather when high winds or waves are expected. Ratios of 10:1 or 20:1 (or more) may be required under survival storm conditions. Shorter scope (3:1 or

4:1) can be used when anchoring temporarily with the boat fully crewed. Anglers seldom pay out scope of more than three times the depth.

The most common cause for dragging anchor is lack of scope. Increasing the length of the rode is the first action to take to stop a dragging anchor. Table 3-4 provides guidelines for scope under a variety of conditions. The suggested ratios should be considered as starting points only. Conditions often call for more scope to prevent dragging.

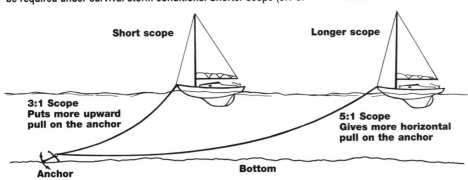

Short scope

Longer scope

3:1 Scope
Puts more upward
pull on the anchor

5:1 Scope
Gives more horizontal
pull on the anchor

Anchor

Bottom

Scope is often expressed as the ratio of the length of anchor rode to the depth of the water. Most situations require a 5:1 to 7:1 scope for good holding.

this happens, the anchor can be prevented from digging into the ground. Holding will be impossible.

- Early Pull–If strain is taken on the rode too early, the pull will be mostly vertical instead of horizontal. Vertical pull dislodges the anchor and causes it to drag across the bottom.

Reverse thrust is used to augment natural forces and help control the boat while rode is being paid out. Send rope overboard fast enough to keep it slack until sufficient scope has been veered. Surging the rope on a cleat or windlass drum is seldom needed after the anchor touches bottom. More often it's necessary to haul rope out of the locker by hand to match the backward movement of the boat. The helmsman should be cautioned not to back down faster than the rode can be veered or the anchor will almost certainly start dragging.

Keeping the anchor lying quietly on the bottom is especially important with Danforth or similar-style anchors. Pressure from the wind and waves can move the boat backward much faster than anticipated. When this happens, the rode comes taut and the anchor can be pulled completely off the bottom. Once free, the flukes may act like a kite and "fly" the anchor up to the surface. Given enough speed, the anchor may actually reach the surface and skip along like a fighting gamefish.

The solution for a "kiting" anchor is obvious: get slack into the rode so the hook falls back to the bottom. This often requires innovative seamanship. A small amount of forward power may slow the backward drift. Short bursts of forward gear at idle speed are usually enough to get the job done. Keep a sharp lookout to make sure the boat does not begin to override the rode, which could result in its becoming tangled in the propeller.

Soft Mud Problems

Patent anchors (Danforths and similar designs) may have trouble digging into a soft mud bottom. Although this seems paradoxical, the reason is the softness of the mud. The crown of the anchor simply sinks into the mud instead of doing its job to rotate the flukes into their proper "digging" position. If this happens, try using a short scope (under 3:1) when setting the anchor. The slightly vertical pull of the rode may help rotate the flukes into their proper orientation for digging into the bottom.

Consider purchasing a special mud anchor if you regularly drop the hook into soft bottoms. Mud anchors have larger flukes of special shape that help the anchor bury itself in soft material. The Fortress anchor with special *mud palms* set at a 45-degree angle is among the best in soft conditions. The traditional favorites of cruising sailors, CQR and Bruce anchors, are not recommended for mud.

Setting the anchor involves putting intentional strain on the rode to pull the flukes deep into the bottom. This is done only after veering scope of at least three times the water depth. If possible, wait until scope exceeds five times the depth before attempting to set the hook. Have the foredeck crew secure the rope to a mooring cleat or bitt and then stand well clear. Continue backing down slowly until the rode becomes taut. If the anchor is properly set, the boat will come sharply head-to. Bubbles from the propeller will appear to be passing the hull

The Flying Fluke

The natural ability of a stockless anchor to "kite" through the water has been exploited by the designer of the Flying Fluke anchor. This anchor literally pulls itself away from the boat as it descends through the water. Outward horizontal movement of the Flying Fluke allows setting an anchor at some distance from the boat. On the bottom, the geometry of the anchor changes, allowing it to penetrate and hold.

Table 3-4

PURPOSE	ANCHOR	SCOPE	NOTES
Typical Scope for Various One-Anchor Situations			
Fishing in Protected Water	Lunch Hook	3:1 or less	Temporary anchoring to stay over fish.
Swimming Off Boat	Lunch Hook	3:1 to 5:1	Temporary anchoring with boat occupied. Calm water.
Floating Lunch	Lunch Hook	3:1 to 5:1	Temporary anchoring with boat occupied. Calm water.
Afternoon Ashore	Working Anchor	5:1 to 7:1	Boat unoccupied. Good holding ground. Protected anchorage.
Sleeping Overnight	Working Anchor	5:1 to 7:1	Crew aboard. Good holding ground. Protected anchorage.
Sleeping Overnight, Foul Weather	Storm Anchor	7:1 to 10:1 (or more)	Crew aboard. Good holding ground. Protected anchorage.
Overnight Ashore	Storm Anchor	7:1 to 10:1	No crew aboard. Boat must fend for itself. Fair weather.

from the stern toward the bow.

Heavy anchors such as plows usually bury themselves with the first real strain. Lighter anchors, especially those made of aluminum, may need to be gently persuaded into the bottom. Symptoms of a dragging anchor include:

• Boat fails to come sharply head-to

• Strong vibrations are felt through anchor rode

• Boat backs out of intended anchoring zone

Veering additional scope is the quickest solution for an anchor that's dragging because it hasn't penetrated into the bottom. Use a short burst of forward thrust to take sternway off the vessel. Veer a sizable amount of anchor line (at least equal to half the depth). The intent is to allow the rode to go completely slack while the boat gathers natural sternway from wind and waves. A slack rode allows the geometry of the anchor to reposition the flukes for best penetration of the bottom the next time the rope is put under strain. Belaying and releasing the rode several times may be necessary before the flukes dig deeply into the bottom.

An anchor that does not hold properly and cannot be made to hold is usually fouled with weeds, mud, a rock, or shells. In all cases, it must be cleared before another attempt can be made. Raise the anchor to the surface and pull the weeds off by hand. Weed fouling usually repeats itself, so consider moving to better holding ground. Rocks or shells also have to be removed manually. "Sloshing" the anchor at the surface may wash off mud, although thick gumbo must be pulled off one gooey handful at a time. Lower the anchor again after it is clean.

Once the anchor is properly dug into the bottom, apply increased reverse thrust until the strain exceeds any anticipated natural forces of wind and waves. A hand on the strained rode should reveal it to be taut, but quiet. Vibrations in the rope often signal movement of the anchor along the bottom. If the boat continues pointing sharply at the anchor and the bubbles continue passing the hull as before, there is reasonable assurance the anchor is holding.

A nylon rode will have stretched considerably while setting the anchor. Expect the boat to surge forward a short distance after the engines are shut down. This surge is caused by the nylon fibers regaining their original, shorter length. Double-check the mooring bitt or cleat to be sure the rope is properly belayed.

Anchoring by the Stern

Anglers often find it more convenient to anchor by the stern. This avoids time lost going forward to handle the ground tackle. While stern anchoring is efficient from a fishing standpoint, it's dangerous seamanship. The bow of a boat is built with reserve buoyancy so it can rise up and over waves. Sterns of powerboats are as flat as a brick wall. Waves striking a flat stern do not raise the boat up. Instead, they break and plunge into the cockpit. This explains why sinkings caused by stern anchoring are common.

WEIGHING ANCHOR

Getting the anchor off the bottom and back on deck always takes more work than putting it out. Muscle power does this work on the majority of boats, especially those under thirty feet. This makes crew safety critical. Whenever possible the crew hauling the line should be sitting with legs apart and feet well braced. This position allows the muscles of the back and arms to develop full power and reduces the possibility of losing balance and being tossed overboard by an unexpected wave.

This vertical drum winch handles both rope and chain. It has an integral, hooded chain pipe. It is available in both manual and electric versions. *(Courtesy Simpson Lawrence)*

If the boat is equipped with a winch or windlass, several wraps of anchor line are taken around the drum to ensure plenty of friction between the rope and drum. Friction transmits power from the windlass to the anchor rode. The operator should take a well-braced position suitable for tailing the rope that comes off the windlass. So far as possible, the operator should not be in a direct line with the rope in case it breaks. The recoil of a parted nylon rope can have the nasty impact of a bullwhip.

Pulling the boat forward to the anchor is the hard way to go. It tires out human muscles and strains electrical winches. Much easier is motoring slowly toward the anchor, hauling in rode as the boat advances. The foredeck crew must work quickly to prevent the boat from overriding the rode, but the total effort from human or electric muscles is much less. Shift into neutral when the rode comes "up and down" (vertical) and secure the rode. Allow the boat to coast over the spot where the anchor lies so that pull from the anchor line is upward and slightly backward. The anchor should break out easily.

The normal heaving (up and down) motion of the bow can be used to coax an anchor out of the ground. Haul in short when the bow goes down and surge the line under a mooring cleat. (There is seldom time to belay it correctly, although that works best.) As the bow heaves upward it exerts dozens of times more force on the rode than is possible with human muscles. Repeat the process three or four times to get the anchor to break out of the bottom.

Expect the flukes to bring up a large sample of the muck, mud, or weeds. Marl, mud, and grass love to attach themselves to anchors. This mess has to be removed before the anchor is brought on deck. A variety of techniques work to clean fouled flukes.

SLOSHING

Lightweight anchors can be sloshed up and down in the water to knock off mud and weeds. Bringing the anchor above the surface and allowing it to splash down seems to provide the best washing action. Use caution to avoid banging the anchor into the side of the hull.

BACKING DOWN

Belay the rode so the anchor hangs just below the waterline. Back down slowly. Dragging the anchor through the water creates the cleansing action. Done properly, this maneuver prevents the sharp flukes from digging into the gel coat, but the dangers of backing while dragging an anchor are obvious. Allow all sternway to come off the boat before hoisting the anchor aboard.

WASHDOWN PUMP

A pump can be rigged to pump raw seawater through a deck spigot. Use a hose to direct the stream onto the flukes of the anchor to remove the debris.

MESSY MANUAL METHOD

Stiff mud defies all attempts to wash it off. The only way to get it off the flukes is to pull great handfuls of muck off the anchor and toss them overboard. This job is messy. Have a bucket of water ready for hand washing. It will take several bucketfuls to rinse mud off the foredeck.

4

ADVANCED ANCHORING TECHNIQUES

While most of the time anchoring can be described as "routine," there are occasions when things don't go quite as expected. In addition, some situations may require special techniques such as a Mediterranean moor or multiple anchors.

SWINGING ROOM

A boat at anchor never sits perfectly still. Rather, it "swings" in an arc around its anchor. The radius of this arc is slightly less than the amount of scope paid out. Maintaining enough swinging room is an important part of anchoring. More than one anchorage has been turned into a pile of tangled boats and angry skippers by an unexpected wind shift. Consideration must be given both to other boats and to nearby obstructions onshore.

Checking for sufficient swinging room is a critical part of the initial reconnoitering of any potential anchorage. Some things to look for include:

• Other Boats—How many are there in the harbor? Try to estimate the amount of scope they

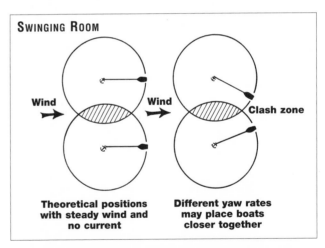

SWINGING ROOM

Wind

Wind

Clash zone

Theoretical positions with steady wind and no current

Different yaw rates may place boats closer together

Boats swing in a large circle centered on their anchors. Different yaw rates can cause boats to swing into one another despite a steady wind. The possibility of collisions is greatest when the wind shifts and the boats struggle to reposition themselves.

are using as a gauge of their swinging room.

• Types of Moorings—Are the boats riding to a single anchor? Or are they using multiple

anchors to reduce swinging room? You will want to follow the pattern set for the anchorage.

• Obvious Incompetence—Is there one boat in the anchorage that is obviously not anchored correctly? (The crew of this boat is usually ashore on a spree.) Stay away from such a vessel as it always spells trouble.

Geometry seems to prove that boats can be anchored quite close to one another without danger of overlapping. After all, they all will be affected by the same wind and current, so should swing around their anchors in concert. This is not what happens, however. No two boats respond to wind and current in the same manner. As a result, the only perfectly safe anchorage is one in which the swinging circles of the boats do not overlap. This ideal situation seldom exists, but experienced sailors always keep as much swinging room as possible.

Using stern anchors is a quick and easy way to limit swinging where full room is not available. This is the solution chosen by most boats in transient anchorages where stays are limited to overnight. A Mediterranean moor is a better choice if the boat will remain anchored for several days. It allows the boat to swing into changing winds or currents while a stern anchor prohibits this natural action.

DRAGGING ANCHOR

Your anchor may hold well long enough to win your confidence and then begin to drag across the bottom. Or it may hold for several hours before beginning to drag. A slowly dragging anchor gives little or no notice of its occurrence. You may be oblivious to it for several hours until the boat has dragged enough to cause a dis-

Table 4-1

Solutions for Dragging Anchor

Problem	Initial Action to Solve
Anchor Will Not Hold on First Attempt	Retrieve anchor and check for fouling. Remove weeds or mud from flukes. Make another approach and relower anchor.
Anchor Will Not Hold After Several Attempts	If several attempts are made and the anchor refuses to hold, the problem is likely the bottom. Move to another location and begin procedure again.
Slow Dragging (After Being Set)	Most likely cause is lack of scope. Veer more rode and observe. Repeat several times as needed. Anchor should begin to hold. If not, retrieve and check for fouled flukes.
Fast Dragging (After Being Set)	Fouled flukes are the likely cause. This often happens in soft mud. Veer more rode. If this does not work, retrieve anchor and check for fouling.
Sudden Breakout (No Holding)	Usually the result of insufficient rode and increasing winds or stormy conditions. Veering more rode seldom causes anchor to reset. Solution is to retrieve and reset anchor. Veer more rode than the first time.

crepancy in your anchor bearings.

However, if the anchor has completely broken free of the bottom or is dragging rapidly, there are several signs:

• Head Falls Off—The boat no longer heads into the wind and waves, but begins yawing widely.

• Sudden Rolling—With the head no longer into the waves, the boat can be caught somewhat sideways. This causes a noticeable increase in rolling.

• Change in Sound—Halyards that had been quiet may begin to snap against the mast. Other rigging that had been noisy will quiet down as the angle of the wind over the bow changes. There may be differences in the sound of the sea or the subtle noises within the hull.

Table 4-1 illustrates typical actions to stop an anchor from dragging. Every situation is unique and the suggested solution may not always work. Paying out additional scope is always the first action to take if the anchor begins dragging after having once been set. Pay out line as fast as the boat can take up the additional slack. Increase the scope by at least the depth of the water before belaying. Wait a few minutes to see if the anchor is still dragging.

In any case, if the anchor cannot be set with a 10:1 scope, the prudent sailor looks for another anchorage. A sleepless night at sea is infinitely preferable to pounding to death on the rocks of a lee shore.

Foul Weather

Severe weather conditions can overpower the

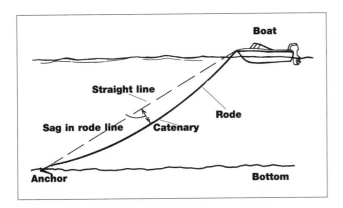

Catenary is the term for the natural sag in the anchor rode between the boat and the anchor. Veering more rode increases the catenary, while shortening the rode decreases it.

The Importance of the Catenary

The word *catenary* describes the natural sag in the anchor rode between the boat and the anchor. This sag takes the form of a sweeping curve and is a natural result of stretching a rope (or chain) between two fixed points. Veering more scope tends to increase the catenary, while shortening the rode decreases it.

While catenary is a natural occurrence, it proves to be beneficial for several reasons. First, it allows the rode to pull more horizontally near the bottom. This increases the holding power of the anchor. And the catenary acts as a natural shock absorber as the boat surges against its rode. By absorbing shock loads, it prevents the anchor from being jerked out of the bottom.

best anchor and cause it to pull out of the best holding ground. Veering more rode is the first step to prevent dragging, but there is a limit to the amount of rode carried aboard. Three additional actions to increase holding power may be tried in this situation:

MOTORING ON THE ANCHOR

This involves operating slow ahead propulsion to relieve some, but not all, of the strain on the anchor rode. The rudder may be used to reduce yawing around the anchor. (Twin-screw boats should maneuver on their engines.) Do not attempt to relieve all strain from the rode as the boat may override it and tangle the rope in a propeller.

Motoring on the anchor can be effective, but only for as long as the fuel supply allows. It's a slim possibility, but sometimes motoring on the anchor for ten minutes to an hour will allow the anchor to reset itself and dig into the bottom sufficiently to hold on its own.

SENTINEL OR KELLET

Known by both names, a sentinel is simply a weight sent about halfway down the rode to improve its catenary. This produces a more horizontal pull on the anchor, increasing its holding power.

A second anchor can be jury-rigged into an emergency sentinel. Use a short loop of chain to attach it to the anchor rode. Tie a light line to the second anchor and send the whole works sliding down the rode. Adjust the light line to position the sentinel about halfway from the boat to the working anchor.

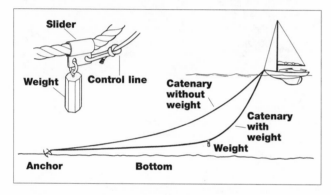

A sentinel (or kellet) improves anchor performance by making the pull on the anchor more horizontal. Commercial fittings that ride on the rode are available, but a large shackle or loop of chain will work in a pinch.

Marine stores sell special bronze fittings designed to eliminate the inevitable chafe on the anchor rode from a chain sentinel. These fittings are meant to be used in conjunction with a large sounding lead or some other cast metal weight. A control line is used to adjust the sentinel's position along the anchor rode. Sentinels must be retrieved before the working anchor can be hauled aboard.

MID-RODE BUOY

The mid-rode buoy works on completely the opposite principle from the sentinel. The buoy creates a reverse catenary in the rode, reducing the upward pull of the boat on the rode as it heaves itself over

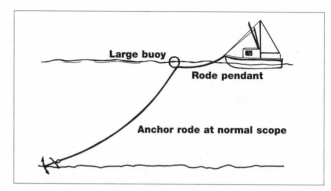

A mid-rode buoy can also be used to increase the holding power of an anchor. It reduces the vertical pull on the anchor of the boat.

the waves. The buoy brings the rode to the surface, so pull from the boat is nearly horizontal. Reducing upward pull from the boat on the anchor allows it to stay dug into the bottom.

A mid-rode buoy is inserted between two sections of anchor rope using shackles. Eyes at either end of the buoy are connected together with a thick steel rod. This rod carries the stress, instead of the softer buoyant material. The length of rode between the anchor and the buoy should be at least seven times the depth.

Putting out a second anchor is another way of reducing dragging. Several ways to accomplish this will be discussed later in this chapter.

UNSTICKING A STUCK ANCHOR

Short Scope

An anchor that has been digging its way into the bottom for a day or longer may become so deeply buried that it resists all efforts at retrieval. This is especially true if there have been high winds, strong currents, or both. Heaving the anchor directly out of the mud seldom works, but there is a trick. You can make the anchor work itself loose while getting ready for sea.

Shorten scope to under 3:1 about a half hour before your planned departure. Detail a lookout to be sure the anchor does not break free prematurely without notice. In most cases, the upward tug from the boat on such short scope will slowly pull the anchor to the top of the mud, making the final breakout that much easier.

Circling the Anchor

Bottom conditions sometimes defy all efforts to dislodge the anchor. Motoring straight forward might help, but is likely to foul a propeller. Instead, reduce scope to less than 3:1 and motor in a wide circle *around* the anchor. When the boat circles upwind (or upcurrent) of the hook, the pull on the rode should move the anchor backward so the flukes come out of the bottom. It may take two or three circles to dislodge an anchor tightly wedged in rocks. Use caution at all times to avoid tangling the rode in a propeller. Making circles is the primary method of extracting an anchor wedged into rocks or caught on some other bottom obstruction.

Buoyant Anchor Retrieval

This method is popular among small groups of professional fishermen, but is otherwise almost unknown. It involves the use of a buoy and a slip ring to increase the vertical pull on the rode. As would be expected, vertical pull is "unfair" to the flukes and causes them to break out of the bot-

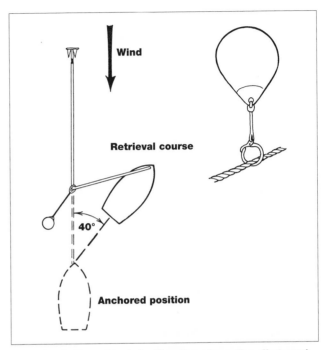

Buoyant anchor retrieval significantly reduces the effort needed to hoist ground tackle. The buoy is clipped around the rode and then deployed overboard. The boat motors forward at an angle of 40 degrees, pulling the buoy under water. Buoyancy of the buoy floats ground tackle to the surface once the anchor breaks loose.

tom. The buoy must have sufficient buoyancy to support the weight of the anchor. A round, inflated vinyl fender works well at this job and can still be used for its original purpose.

Buoyant anchor retrieval has several advantages. First, it does not require a large crew. That's why this technique is a favorite of professional fishermen working alone at sea. It also requires minimal effort by human muscles to get the ground tackle back aboard. You don't need a "deck ape" to haul the rode aboard with brute force. Finally, it's a relatively quick method of hoisting anchor.

A slip ring with the buoy attached is clipped over the anchor rode and the buoy sent over the side.

Table 4-2

Buoyant Anchor Retrieval Buoy Selection Chart	
ANCHOR WEIGHT	BUOY SIZE
To 24 lbs.	12" diameter
24 to 56 lbs.	15" diameter
56 to 100 lbs.	18" diameter
100 to 150 lbs.	21" diameter

Anchor weight includes chain and rope.
Table courtesy Bos'n Manufacturing Co.

The boat is then run ahead at 30 to 40 degrees off the wind. This movement of the boat pulls the buoy forward and *downward* toward the anchor. The buoy actually submerges and is pulled to the bottom. Continue motoring forward until the buoy is pulled all the way down to the anchor. At this point, the pull of the boat helps twist the anchor out of the bottom. Once the anchor is broken free, the buoy floats it to the surface. The floating ground tackle aboard is easily pulled aboard.

This idea is not new. Crude, homemade versions have been used by generations of fishermen. Several devices have been patented in recent years to make the job easier. One is made of plastic, the others of noncorrosive metal. All except one have moving parts subject to wear or breakage.

The best buoyant retrieval device is the Yanchor by Bos'n Manufacturing Co. It's a simple open ring of stainless steel wire. A rope pendant is spliced to an eye at one end of the open loop. The other end of the loop is formed into a crook. There are no moving parts to break. In use, the rope pendant is attached to the buoy. The ring is then slipped over the anchor rode and the pendant jerked into the crook of the ring. This makes the Yanchor completely captive on the anchor rode.

The buoyant method of anchor retrieval obviously raises the possibility of running over the rode with the boat. This could result in a fouled propeller. One way of avoiding this problem is to cleat the anchor rode off the stern just as the boat begins moving forward. (Never anchor off the stern, as a swamped boat may be the result.)

Reversing Out an Anchor

Soft mud or loose sand bottoms do not always require circling around the anchor. If the hook won't break out when the rode is "up and down," secure the rope to the mooring bitt or cleat. Begin slowly increasing reverse power until the anchor breaks loose. Once it's free, immediately use a short burst of forward thrust to take sternway off the boat. The foredeck crew should now be able to haul the anchor aboard.

Reversing out an anchor should never be done without due consideration for the strain it puts on the boat, the deck fittings, and the ground tackle. The only advantage to this method is that it doesn't strain the muscles (and heart) of the person working the foredeck. It also is not likely to result in fouling the propeller. Use reverse power to break out an anchor *only* if the mooring bitt or cleat is of extremely stout construction and has been through-bolted to the deck with a large backing plate. Crew members should stand well clear of the rode while it is under strain. Use this method only in soft mud or sand. It will not work in rocks, where a broken rope or a bent fluke is sure to result.

Scowing the Anchor

There are times when your anchor is almost certain to become stuck in the bottom. Fouled

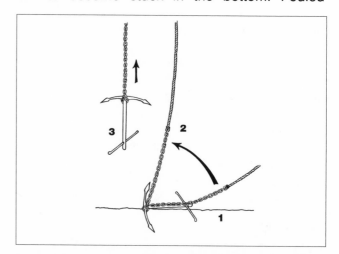

Scowing an anchor allows it to be pulled out backward should it become fouled in the bottom. The anchor rode is attached to the crown of the anchor. A lashing holds it in place on the shank while anchored. Any unfair pull on the rode breaks the lashing and allows the anchor to be retrieved.

anchors are expected in rocky areas where they routinely jam in crevices or beneath large boulders. *Scowing* (also called *becuing* or *crowning*) is the time-honored way of preventing the loss of an anchor under these conditions. It's not a method of retrieval, but rather is that famous "ounce of prevention" practiced before the anchor is lowered.

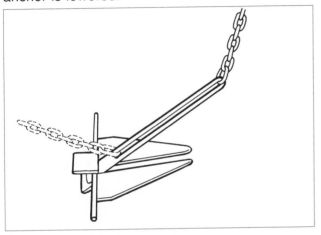

Sliding-ring anchors are essentially self-scowing. While handy for fishing or a quick lunch, they should not be used for overnight anchoring. A wind shift can cause the ring to slide and the anchor to break out of the bottom.

An anchor is scowed when the rode is permanently attached to the crown instead of the shank. This attachment obviously prevents the anchor from working unless the rode is led upward from the crown along the shank where it is temporarily secured with a few wrappings of light twine. These wrappings are made in the way of the shackle at the top of the shank. A scowed anchor digs into the bottom in the normal fashion. The light twine lashings are under little or no strain because the pull on the rode is parallel to the shank.

When the anchor is retrieved, up-and-down pull on the rode causes the twine lashings to break. The rode is now attached only to the crown of the anchor, so pull from the rode is now the reverse of the way the anchor is hooked into the rocks.

Several manufacturers offer what might be called "self-scowing" anchors. Nearly all of these designs have shanks made out of metal rod bent into a U-shape. A large steel ring is held captive in this U. When the boat is anchored, the ring slides to the top of the shank as in a regular anchor. However, if the anchor becomes stuck in

The Anchor Saver is a mechanical scowing device that replaces undependable twine lashings. The rode is held to the shank by a metal clip until dislodged by a special tubular weight.

the bottom, running over top of the anchor causes the ring to slide down the shank to the crown. This reverses the pull and allows the anchor to be pulled out backward.

Anchor Saver, Inc., has an interesting mechanical scowing device that replaces the twine with a metal-to-metal connection. It is a highly specialized pelican hook designed to clip on to any fiber rode. In use, the boat is brought directly over the fouled anchor. A special weight supplied with the Anchor Saver device is clipped around the rode and allowed to slide down. The impact of this weight causes the pelican hook to spring open, releasing the rode from the shank. The rode is now attached only to the crown of the anchor, allowing it to be pulled out backward.

Scowing is never suggested for storm anchors or for times when the boat will be left unattended. Bottom conditions can chafe or break the twine lashings. If this happens, all holding power of the anchor is lost as it pulls out backward. Scowed anchors are most useful when fishing or for other temporary needs.

Buoyed Trip Line

A buoyed trip line allows the anchor to be pulled out backward, but does not present the dangers of unexpected release inherent in scowing. The trip line is tied to the crown of the anchor prior to lowering. It is carried to the surface by a small buoy (often a vinyl boat fender). The length of the trip line is just slightly more than the depth of the water at high tide. If the anchor becomes fouled in the bottom, the trip line allows it to be pulled out backward.

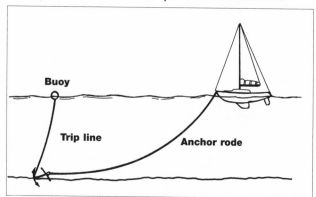

Attaching a buoyed trip line to the crown is another way of recovering a fouled anchor. The trip line allows it to be pulled out backward while the buoy marks the location of the anchor.

Accept the Inevitable

Anchors sometimes get so wedged in the bottom that no amount of huffing and puffing will break

them free. This is common in rocky conditions when the anchor has been under severe strain for an extended period. When it happens, accept the fact and cut loose the offending ground tackle. Bring the boat to a position directly over top of the recalcitrant anchor before cutting the rode. This minimizes the loss of rope. Without a diver, there's little that can be done about the shackles and chain left on the bottom attached to the anchor.

On rare occasions, a diver may be able to free the anchor. Diving is no sure cure, however. A person working underwater does not have the leverage to dislodge an anchor that is tightly wedged in rocks. Often the best a diver can do is to unshackle the chain so it can be retrieved along with an uncut rope. Divers without air tanks are seldom able to perform any serious work on the bottom. Their limited air supply only allows simple reconnaissance, but this may prove valuable in planning maneuvers of the boat to pull the anchor out.

CREW COMMUNICATIONS

Shouting and yelling is the mark of an inexperienced crew and an unprepared skipper. Disciplined crews learn a simple set of hand signals that allow communication between helm and foredeck without loud voices. Hand signals are not done for show. They have an entirely practical purpose. Wind, engine noise, and even sounds from shore can make it difficult or impossible to understand spoken words from one end of the boat to the other. Hand signals avoid costly misunderstandings.

There is no universal set of pleasure-boat hand signals for anchoring. Every crew is free to make up its own. In devising your signals, keep in mind that they should require only one hand. The person giving a signal may be using the other hand to hold on to the boat or to handle equipment. Here are a few suggestions:

From Helm to Foredeck

These signals allow the skipper to communicate with the foredeck.

- Let Go (Lower Anchor)—arm extended straight forward from body, index finger pointed down toward deck. Make vigorous downward pointing motion with hand and forearm.

- Hoist (Weigh Anchor)—elbow bent and forearm extended upward, index finger pointed up toward sky. Make vigorous upward pointing motion with hand and arm.

- Belay (Secure Rode to Bitt)—arm extended straight forward from body, hand made into fist. Make sweeping horizontal movement of fist parallel to deck, bending arm at elbow.

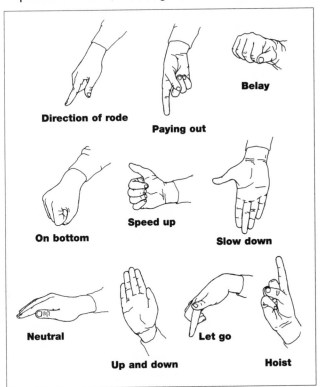

From Foredeck to Helm

These signals allow the foredeck crew to pass information back to the helm. They fall into two categories: lowering and raising the anchor.

Lowering Anchor

- Paying Out (Rode Being Veered)—arm extended at downward angle to side of body, index finger pointed down toward deck. Make vigorous pointing motion with hand and arm.

- On Bottom (Anchor Is on the Bottom)—make fist. Use whole arm for downward punching action toward deck.

- Belay (Rode Is Secure on Bitt)—arm extended to side of body, hand made into fist. Make sweeping horizontal movement of fist parallel to deck by bending arm at elbow.

- Direction of Rode from Boat—use whole arm and hand to make large pointing motion in direction rode lies from the boat. Repeat motion several times.

Raising Anchor

- Direction of Rode from Boat—same as above.

- Speed Up (Motion of Boat Through Water)—hand made into fist with thumb extended upward and forearm vertical. Make upward pointing motion with thumb.

- Slow Down (Motion of Boat Through Water)—hand flat, palm toward viewer. Arm extended downward. Make pushing motion with palm and arm toward viewer.

• Neutral (Shift into Neutral)—arm extended to side of body, hand open with palm down. Make sweeping horizontal movement of palm parallel to deck by bending arm at elbow.

• Up and Down (Anchor Is Directly Beneath Bow, Rode Taut)—open hand extended upward with forearm vertical. Make up-and-down motion with arm and hand as if pointing at sky.

Hand signal motions must be crisp and exaggerated. Watch an experienced cop directing traffic through a major intersection to see how exaggeration makes hand signals easier to understand. (That's also why many traffic cops wear white gloves, to make their hands stand out.) Big gestures aren't likely to be confused with an involuntary twitch or other meaningless motion.

Mouth Whistle Signals

Blasts on a mouth whistle can be used to call attention to hand signals, especially those from the skipper. Or the whistle can eliminate the need for hand signals by creating a private code similar to this one:

1 Short Blast—lower the anchor or pay out additional line.

2 Short Blasts—raise the anchor or haul in line.

3 Short Blasts—anchor is up and down.

1 Long Blast—belay.

These signals should be exchanged *only* on plastic mouth whistles and *never* on the ship's horn. This avoids confusing nearby vessels who might think a private anchor signal is a maneuvering signal under the Rules of the Road. (All of the above signals have distinct meanings under the Rules of the Road when given on the boat's main horn.)

Electronic Communication

For less than thirty dollars, Radio Shack sells a hands-free set of FM walkie-talkies. They come complete with a headset containing an earphone and boom microphone. The transmitter and battery are located on a belt pack. A VOX (voice actuated) circuit switches the transmitter on when the wearer talks. This eliminates the need to operate a push-to-talk button.

When anchoring, the skipper and the foredeck crew each wear one of these walkie-talkies. They talk back and forth as necessary to exchange information. The only difficulty comes if one person is long-winded. The person transmitting cannot be interrupted by the receiver. Once the VOX circuit actuates, the talker's receiver is shut off. Walkie-talkie users have to learn to keep conversations short and to spend more time listening than talking.

ANCHORING UNDER SAIL

Blow boaters are not required to furl their sails and start the "iron main" to anchor. The procedure can be done entirely under sail. And, in fact, coming to anchor under sail is the mark of a skilled sailor. Success is dependent upon thorough preparation, with even small oversights causing enormous problems. Among the things to prepare are:

• Anchor Rode—must be led clear of all shrouds, stays, lifeline stanchions, and pulpits. Fouling the rode around the bow pulpit is a major cause of anchoring difficulties on sailboats.

- Headsails—should be lowered and stowed out of the way of the foredeck crew. Pay particular attention to headsail sheets, which often become tangled in the anchor rode. Keep the pointed flukes and the ends of the anchor stock away from the sail to avoid rips.

- Mainsail—Uncoil the main halyard and fake it down in preparation for rapid lowering of the mainsail. Check that the mainsheet is clear and free to run.

- Engine—Even though you are not planning to use power, have your engine running in neutral. The rumble of an auxiliary may signal an embarrassing end to your attempt to anchor under sail, but it may be the safest, most seamanlike way to get out of trouble.

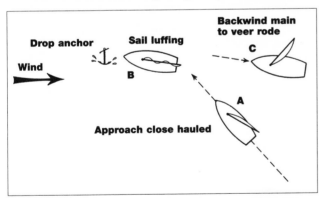

When anchoring under sail, approach under close-hauled main only (A). At the drop spot turn head-to-wind (B) and allow the sail to luff. Drop the anchor when forward motion ceases. If possible, backwind the main by pushing the boom out (C) to cause the boat to move backward as rode is paid out.

If the anchorage is not crowded, it pays to sail through the planned drop zone to test both the wind and current. The best anchorages are protected by trees or land topography that can produce unusual wind conditions. The direction of the wind may change dramatically or it may disappear completely.

The classic approach under sail is to close-reach under mainsail alone to the drop zone as shown at A in the illustration. Turn head-to-wind and allow the boat to coast to a stop at B with the mainsail luffing. Lower the anchor smartly to the bottom. Don't expect the boat to remain stopped for more than an instant. Wind pressure on both the luffing mainsail and the rest of the rigging will cause it to begin to gather sternway. On smaller boats, this sternway can be augmented by pushing the boom out to backwind the mainsail as shown at C.

Anchor rode is paid out as the boat backs away until appropriate scope (about 4:1) for setting the anchor has been veered. Secure the rode to allow the boat to pull sharply on it to set the anchor in the bottom. Then veer additional rode necessary to achieve the required riding scope.

Different methods are required when the wind is too light to achieve more than bare steerageway. One possibility is to approach the drop zone by running downwind. At the appropriate moment, lower the anchor smartly with the vessel still moving. Pay out enough scope to set the anchor before cleating the rode to bring the vessel head-to-wind. The helmsman turns the rudder to assist the vessel in coming to the wind. Veer additional riding scope. A downwind approach of this type is normally done under headsail (genoa) alone with the mainsail furled. It requires a great deal of skill and some luck to accomplish safely.

The majority of modern sailboats have deep fin keels with their rudders separated and well aft. This configuration poses a danger when anchoring. Under some conditions, the vessel may swing over its rode in such a way that the rope becomes trapped between the fin and the rudder. This is a real danger when attempting a downwind approach. If it happens, a vessel

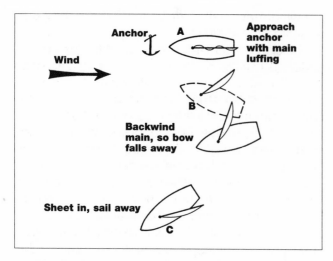

To sail off an anchor, the main is allowed to luff while the boat is hauled up to the anchor (A). Once the anchor breaks loose, backwind the main so the bow falls off (B). Sheet in and begin to sail away (C).

caught this way will ride stern-to instead of head-to-wind. Worse, the strains of anchoring will be transmitted to the rather fragile rudder and steering gear. In calm weather a diver may be able to force the rode off the tip of the rudder. In heavy weather, however, it may be necessary to slip the rode and set a new anchor. Recovery of the original anchor and rode is problematic.

Getting under way under sail is another exercise in seamanship. If wind and currents allow, the vessel should be hauled to short scope (under 3:1) before the mainsail is hoisted. With the main luffing, continue hauling the rode until the anchor breaks free at A in the illustration above. Manually backwinding the main at B causes the bow to fall away from the wind. After if falls off, let the main fill and sail away while the foredeck crew completes recovery of the anchor.

Hauling the boat up to the anchor may not be possible in heavy winds or strong currents. Instead, try tacking the vessel up to the anchor

under mainsail alone. Haul in the rode as the vessel moves forward. This is a tricky maneuver that requires skill both at the helm and on the foredeck. It's best done on vessels equipped with a winch or windlass. Hauling by hand may result in rope burns or pinched fingers if the helmsman misses a tack.

Catamaran Sailboats

A catamaran has need for special anchoring techniques because its two hulls allow no mooring post or anchor cleat on the boat's exact centerline. A rope bridle must be rigged from the rode to the bows of both hulls. The legs of this bridle must be at least twice as long as the distance between the hulls. If the bridle legs are too short, the pull from the rode will tend to "pinch" the bows of the hulls together and put undue strain on the bridging between them. Also, the legs must be of equal length or the boat will not lie squarely into the wind.

It's impractical to splice up a special bridle because the scope needed changes with each anchorage. Instead, pay out the required scope from the bow of one hull. Attach a short line from the other hull to the rode with a rolling hitch and let out more rode until the required bridle is formed.

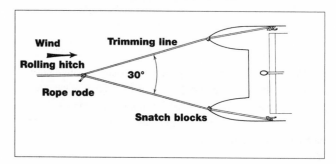

A bridle is necessary to properly anchor a catamaran. The rode is paid off the bow of one hull. After sufficient rode has been paid out, a second line is attached to it with a rolling hitch. The two lines are adjusted to control the angle at which the boat rides the winds or waves.

Adjusting either leg of the bridle squares the boat into the wind or waves.

Catamarans are often sailed off the beach. The frustrating process of getting back into deep water through a surf can be eliminated by dropping a kedge anchor set as the boat is sailed onto the beach. Drop the kedge at least 150 to 200 feet offshore, then sail onto the beach as usual. The rode remains slack while the boat is onshore. Getting back into deep water is a matter of hauling on the kedge rode until the boat is pulled beyond the surf.

SETTING THE ANCHOR WATCH

Anchoring is not an event that ends with the setting of the hook. Rather, it is a process that continues as long as the boat is riding to the anchor, whether for two hours, two days, or two weeks. Big ships establish what are called *anchor watches*. The number of crew involved in these watches is substantially reduced from the number on duty when the ships are at sea. Formal anchor watches are seldom established on pleasure boats, but the concept remains valid. Someone must remain responsible for the safety of the boat at all times, even at anchor.

The primary responsibility of the anchor watch is to ensure that the vessel is not dragging. In addition, the rode should be inspected regularly at wear points such as chocks or cleats. The anchor watch must also display the appropriate lights (at night) or sound the appropriate fog signals. Finally, the watch must be alert to other vessels that may be anchoring too close or may be dragging their anchors.

While this sounds like a lot of work, the job can be simplified. Choosing a federally designated anchorage eliminates the need to display anchor lights or sound fog signals (on boats under twenty meters). Electronic navigation equipment such as Loran-C or GPS can give warning if the boat drags from its original location. Under some conditions, the anchor watch might even be done from shore using binoculars.

Anchor Bearings
Anchor bearings are a navigational tool for determining whether the boat is dragging. They are traditionally compass bearings, but these days anchor bearings have gone electronic. Loran-C and GPS receivers can be programmed to sound a warning if the boat drifts too far from its original location. The electronic navigator still takes compass bearings, but only to backstop his microchip marvels.

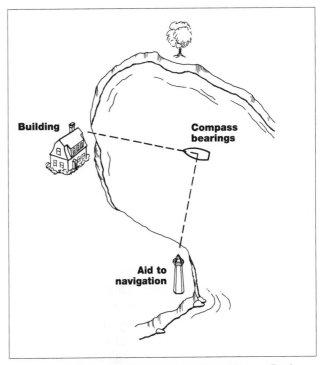

Anchor bearings are visual compass bearings taken on fixed objects to ascertain whether the anchor is holding. For best results, objects should be at least ½ nautical mile from the boat.

73

Visual (Compass) Anchor Bearings

Compass bearings are best taken on two or three objects on land that can be easily recognized both during the day and at night. Two objects are the minimum number needed, while three is optimum. It's important to use fixed objects that will not move. Lighted objects, especially if they are shown on the chart, are best. In remote areas, however, lights can be few and far between. The navigator must use his wits to discover at least two objects that will be visible by moonlight. Typical objects to use include:

- Fixed, lighted aids to navigation

- Houses or buildings, especially with prominent cupolas

- Flagpoles or monuments (likely to be lighted at night)

- Chimneys, water towers, and radio towers

- Trees that are prominent above the treeline or are isolated in otherwise featureless terrain

At least two of the objects should be nearly 90 degrees apart. This ensures that lines of position (LOPs) from them will intersect at approximately right angles. Two or more LOPs that cross in this manner are known as a *fix* by navigators. The angle at which the lines cross determines the accuracy of the fix. A 90-degree crossing provides the smallest area of ambiguity. The ambiguity increases as the angle varies from this optimal crossing.

Objects chosen for visual anchor bearings should be at least half a nautical mile away from the boat. The closer an object lies to the vessel, the less its compass bearing changes if the boat drifts from its original location. Anchor bearings do not have to be plotted on the chart. In fact, it may be

impossible to plot them if the landmarks used are not charted. All that's necessary is to write them in your log book for future reference.

Shoot a round of bearings from time to time while the boat is at anchor. If the new ones differ greatly from the original bearings, that's an indication that the boat has moved from its proper position. The distance of the *offset* (drift) between bearings can be calculated by using the Rule of Sixty. This rule says that *for every degree of difference between the two bearings, the offset is equal to one sixtieth of the distance to the object.* If 2 bearings differ by 3 degrees on an object two nautical miles apart, this rule calculates the offset—or the distance you have drifted—at approximately 600 feet.

$$Offset = \frac{12,152}{60} \times 3$$

$$Offset = 202.53 \times 3$$

$$Offset = 607.6$$

Table 4-3 was developed using the Rule of Sixty. It indicates the predicted amount of offset

Table 4-3

Predicted Boat Movement Based on Bearing Change (predicted offset in feet)					
BEARING CHANGE (DEGREES)	**DISTANCE TO OBJECT SIGHTED (NAUTICAL MILES)**				
	0.5	1.0	1.5	2.0	3.0
0.5	25	51	76	101	152
1.0	51	101	152	203	304
1.5	76	152	228	304	456
2.0	101	203	304	405	608
2.5	127	253	378	506	759
3.0	152	304	456	608	911
5.0	253	506	759	1,012	1,519
7.5	380	759	1,139	1,519	2,278
10.0	506	1,013	1,519	2,025	3,038
(Predicted distances are approximate.)					

(in feet) for angular variations based on the distance to the reference object from the boat.

Drag Alarms

Sailors who sleep "on the hook" have devised a variety of methods to alert them should the anchor begin to drag during the night. Two methods are common. The *crash-and-clatter* method made famous by Joshua Slocum has the low-tech benefit of low cost. A small weight (e.g., a lead line) is lowered to the bottom beneath the boat. Sufficient line is paid out to allow for normal swinging around the anchor. The line from the weight is then looped around a stick that supports a couple of pots and pans, and the bitter end is secured to a cleat. If the boat drifts, the lead weight pulls the line taut. This jerks the prop out from beneath the pots and a loud crash and clatter results.

Electronic devices are the high-tech method of warning the sleeping crew. Procedures for setting an electronic anchor drag alarm vary with brands of equipment. In most cases, the location of the boat at anchor is punched in to the Loran-C or GPS receiver. If the vessel moves away from that spot by more than a predetermined amount, an alarm sounds. It's normal for the operator to select the acceptable limit of movement to accommodate normal swinging on the anchor.

Lights and Signals

Except when anchored in a federally designated anchorage area, pleasure boats at anchor are generally required to display an all-round white light in the fore part of the vessel where it can best be seen. This light should be visible at least two nautical miles and displayed from dusk to dawn. During daylight, a black ball day shape replaces the anchor light.

Boats less than 7 meters in length (about 23 feet) are not required to exhibit anchor lights or shapes when not anchored in or near a narrow channel or where other vessels normally navigate. Boats less than 20 meters (about 65 feet) are not required to display anchor lights or shapes when anchored in Coast Guard–designated special anchorage areas.

Boats anchored in clear visibility are not required to sound fog signals. However, during fog or other times of reduced visibility, the Rules of the Road require anchored boats under 100 meters (about 300 feet) in length to ring a bell. This bell should be rung rapidly for five seconds at intervals of not more than one minute. A vessel of less than 12 meters (about 39 feet) is not obliged to give this signal, but if she does not, she must make some other "efficient sound signal" at intervals of not more than two minutes. As with lights and day shapes, bell signals are not required of vessels under 20 meters anchored in a designated anchorage.

In addition to the bell signal, vessels at anchor are allowed to notify other boats of their location with a special whistle signal. This signal consists of three blasts in succession: one short, one prolonged, and one short. The use of this whistle signal does not supplant the rapid ringing of the bell, which must continue at one-minute intervals.

SPECIAL ANCHORING TECHNIQUES

Anchor Ashore

An anchor does not have to be used underwater. It can be carried ashore and driven into the ground by hand to provide a "deadman" attachment for a mooring line. This is common practice among river cruisers who often tie up for the night to vacant stretches of bank that do not provide other attachment points. Great Lakes gunkholers have found that sending a stern anchor ashore is one way of limiting their boat's swinging room in the snug coves of Lake Huron's fabled North Channel.

Sheldon and LaVerna Johnson grew tired of trying to make conventional anchors work

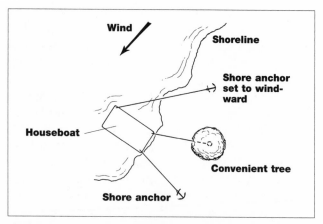

Anchors can be used as "deadmen" on dry land. This is often done by houseboats on inland lakes or when cruising rivers. Anchoring ashore allows the boat to be secured along the bank for overnight rest.

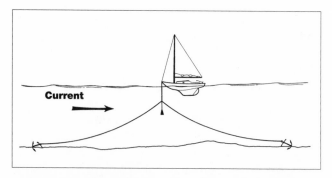

In a Bahamian moor the rodes of two anchors are connected below the surface of the water. A riding pendant rises from this connection to the boat. This arrangement reduces the swinging room required when the current or wind changes.

onshore when they tied up their houseboat for the night. Their solution is a curious blend of a GI entrenching tool and a portable pile driver. Sold under the ShoreFast Anchor brand name, their device allows one person to drive a deadman rope attachment into dirt, sand, or gravel. The holding power is enormous, but the best part of the Johnsons' invention is that the pile driver reverses to pull the ShoreFast Anchor back out of the ground.

Bahamian Moor

This method of anchoring with two anchors was developed for use in areas where the wind (or current) undergoes regular and predictable changes. One anchor is set to the existing situation, the other is set to meet the expected change of wind or current. When the shift comes, the working anchor becomes "lazy" while the other anchor takes the strain.

A simplified Bahamian moor could be done by setting two anchors off the bow (see illustration), but this invites tangled rodes. A better arrange-

ment is to connect the rodes together well below the water and have a single pendant lead upward to the vessel. Boats sailing the tropics often carry special equipment for this arrangement. The Bruce Chain Tensioner is a patented device that simplifies setting a Bahamian moor.

Breast Anchor

Many times it is necessary to spend the night moored on the windward side of a pier. While fenders can protect the hull against damage, their creaking and squealing makes restful sleep impossible. A breast anchor set to windward from amidships will take most of the pressure from the wind and quiet down the fenders enough to allow the crew to get some rest.

In most cases the need for a breast anchor does not become apparent until after the boat is fully moored. That's why the common way of setting one is by dinghy. For safety, attach an inflated fender or other float to the anchor with a line equal in length to the depth before sending it down. This makeshift buoy warns other vessels of the presence of an anchor and rode off the side of your boat. The rode from the breast anchor can be led to a midships cleat, but this is not the best

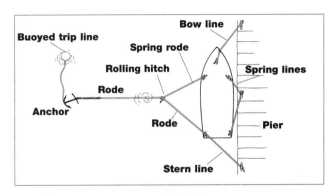

A breast anchor holds the boat away from a pier or bulkhead. Using a spring line as shown allows the angle of the boat to be adjusted. The spring line is attached to the rode with a rolling hitch. A buoyed trip line warns other boats of the anchor and allows easy retrieval.

arrangement. Cleating amidships allows the bow or stern to pivot into the dock and the fender squealing begins. Instead, rig a bridle by tying a short length of line to the rode with a rolling hitch. The rode is then secured to a cleat at the bow of the vessel while the short line goes to a stern cleat. The angle of the boat along the pier can be altered by adjusting the bridle legs.

Double Bow Anchors

Many boats tend to "sail" around their anchors. This is particularly true of shallow-draft power-boats with high topsides. First the boat sheers off to port, and then it swings to starboard under pressure from the wind. This movement, called *yawing*, prevents the anchor from burying itself into the bottom by forcing it to reset with each swing from port to starboard. The classic way to reduce yawing is with two anchors off the bow.

The traditional method of setting two anchors is to drop the main hook and get it well buried. Then, motor to the location where the second anchor will be dropped. While motoring, you must constantly tend the rode from the first

anchor to prevent fouling in the propeller. The second anchor is then dropped and set. Let the boat drift back on both rodes, adjusting them until they are pulling more or less evenly. The angle between the two rodes should be at least 30 degrees and seldom more than 45 degrees.

Avoid setting two anchors in a straight line off the bow. If the boat starts to drag, one anchor may just plow a furrow in the bottom for the other to follow and neither one will hold. Also, never set two anchors off the boat if a major wind shift is expected. Should the boat pivot 180 degrees, the two rodes will become tangled and retrieval will be difficult.

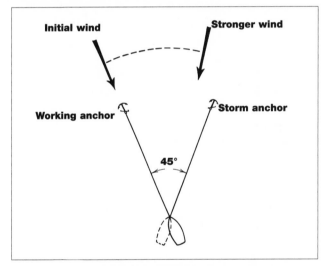

Two anchors set off the bow will reduce yawing. The anchors should be set at an angle of approximately 45 degrees apart. A second anchor also can be set in anticipation of a wind shift. If one anchor is larger, it should be set in the direction of the stronger wind (or current).

Mediterranean Moor

Named for its common use in ports around the Mediterranean Sea, this technique allows the maximum number of boats to use a short pier or quay. An anchor is dropped well off the pier and the vessel is backed into its dock. Spring lines are taken ashore and tension on the anchor rode adjusted to keep the vessel's stern from coming into contact with the pier. Departing is a matter of slipping the spring lines and hauling the vessel out to the anchor, where it may be motored or sailed off.

Although simple in appearance, a Mediterranean moor requires a high degree of seamanship. The anchor must be dropped in the correct position relative to the final docking space. In addition, the vessel must be backed with precision into position along the quay. This often means backing between other moored boats despite crosswinds or currents. Changes in the height of tide must also be monitored. A falling tide can result in a slack rode, allowing the stern of the vessel to grind into the pier.

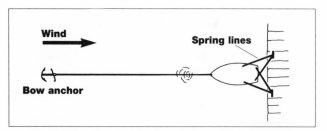

In a Mediterranean moor, a bow anchor is used to prevent the stern from hitting the dock. This anchor is dropped prior to backing into the assigned slip. Crossed stern lines and spring lines are used ashore to keep the boat centered in its dock space.

Stern Anchor, Auxiliary

Another way to reduce yawing on a single bow anchor is to set an auxiliary stern anchor. This is usually a lighter anchor (lunch hook) than the main one set off the bow. There are two methods for setting an auxiliary stern anchor:

METHOD 1

Drop and set the main anchor in the usual fashion. Continue paying out rode until scope reaches ten to eighteen times the depth. Lower the stern anchor. Pull in the bow rode and pay out the stern

rode until the vessel is properly positioned between the two anchors.

METHOD 2

Drop and set the main anchor in the usual fashion. Use a dinghy to carry out the stern anchor and rode. Lower the stern anchor in the appropriate location.

With either method, the scope of the stern anchor must be carefully adjusted to allow the vessel some swing, but to prevent excessive yawing.

Under the Chin

A simple expedient to stop excessive yawing at anchor is to drop a second hook *under the chin*. It is lowered to the bottom directly under the bow and the chain portion of the rode is allowed to pile up next to it. In order to yaw, the vessel must move the weight of the second anchor and chain. Naturally, some movement will happen, but it will be much slower and more comfortable than without the extra hook. Note that an anchor under the chin does not increase the holding power of the main anchor. It only reduces the yawing motion.

ANCHORING TRICKS

Backing the Anchor

Two anchors may be used in tandem on a single rode. In most cases, a smaller anchor is set ahead of the main anchor to increase its holding ability. This technique is known as *backing the anchor*. A variety of methods can be used to connect the two anchors to the rode. The easiest is to shackle the chain for the light anchor to the shank of the main anchor.

While backing the anchor looks easy on paper, it is an extremely difficult maneuver to perform. The two anchors must be laid out carefully on the bot-

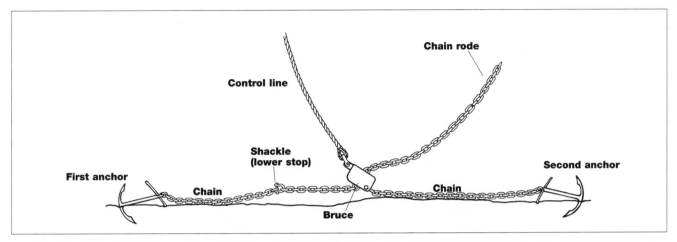

The Bruce Chain Tensioner makes setting a Bahamian moor easy. The device rides down the rode of the first anchor and has the rode of the second anchor attached to it. All-chain rodes are needed for it to work.

tom. If the chain of one tangles around the stock of the other, all holding ability of the tangled anchor will be lost. Also, should the two anchors start to drag, the forward one will plow a furrow for the rear one.

Bruce Chain Tensioner

This simple metal device allows setting two anchors in a Bahamian moor with little fuss. The first anchor is lowered in the normal fashion and the boat allowed to drift to the location where the second anchor will be set. The second is sent down the rode of the first using the Bruce Chain Tensioner. The boat moves forward to a location midway between the two anchors, and the single rode is alternately heaved in and paid out to ratchet the Bruce Chain Tensioner into position on the chain of the first anchor. The boat then pays out the desired amount of scope. Retrieval is facilitated through a buoyed control line.

Freshen the Nip

Even though the anchor rope may pass through a smooth chock or over a roller, there is some inevitable chafe. In time, this chafe can wear

through the best nylon rope. It's doubtful that much damage will be done on a single overnight anchoring. The real problem comes when the boat lies to its anchor for several days (or weeks) at a time. In these cases, it's advisable to "freshen the nip" at regular intervals.

The *nip* is sailor talk for the small area of the rope that is being subjected to chafe. Paying out a foot or so of rope every day ensures that fresh rope is always in the nip. Since chafe damage is cumulative, freshening the nip reduces the impact of serious wear by spreading it over a long stretch of rope.

Rowing Out an Anchor

Additional bow or stern anchors are easiest set with the use of a dinghy. The anchor should not be stowed in the dinghy, but suspended from the stern. This avoids the problem of lifting it over the small boat's gunwale, a maneuver that is likely to capsize the dinghy. Use a light line to hold the anchor. One end is secured to a thwart and the other led through the eye in the shank of the anchor and back to a cleat or other place where it is secured temporarily.

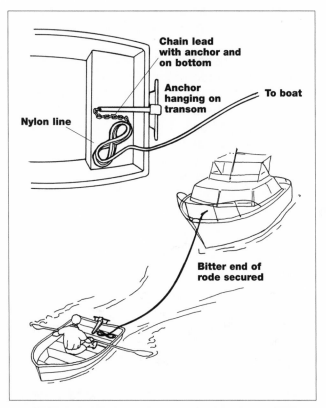

Chain lead
with anchor and
on bottom

Anchor
hanging on
transom

To boat

Nylon line

Bitter end of
rode secured

The anchor rode should be paid out of the dinghy when rowing out an anchor. Suspend the anchor from the stern of the dinghy with a lashing. This avoids lifting heavy ground tackle in a small boat.

Anchor rode equal to the required scope is then faked into the after end of the boat. This allows the rope to pay off the stern of the dinghy as it is rowed away from the big boat. Never attempt to pull the anchor rope off the deck of the big boat. Resistance of the rope in the water will soon overpower the arms of the strongest oarsman. Letting the rope pay out of the dinghy reduces the strain on human muscles, which are taxed enough if there is any wind or sea running.

In the drop zone, the light line securing the

anchor to the stern of the dinghy is let go and the anchor drops to the bottom. The crew on the big boat then adjusts the rode to the proper length while the dinghy returns.

An outboard-powered inflatable boat can also be used to take out an anchor. However, several precautions are necessary. The most obvious is that the propeller of the outboard must never be allowed to come into contact with the anchor rode. Not as obvious is the possibility of damaging one or more of the inflatable's air tubes with the flukes or stock of the anchor. It is not possible to hang the anchor off the stern of an outboard boat because of the motor, so the anchor must be stowed flat in the bottom of the inflatable, a location that brings any of its sharp metal edges into close proximity to the air tubes.

Kedging

Kedging is a method of moving a boat solely through the use of anchors. Two hooks are needed. The vessel is brought to short scope on one while the other is carried ahead the full length of its rode. (See "Rowing Out an Anchor," page 79.) The second anchor is set and the first anchor hauled aboard. Then the vessel is hauled up to the second anchor. This procedure is repeated as often as necessary to move the boat to the desired new position.

Kedging has an honored place in American history. The frigate U.S.S. *Constitution* escaped a fleet of British warships this way during the War of 1812. The incident took place off Little Egg Harbor, New Jersey, on July 17, 1812. The American frigate would have been defeated by the massed guns of the enemy ships except for a daring plan. Captain Isaac Hull used his ship's boats to carry the *Constitution's* massive anchors well forward. Then the crew walked around the capstans, pulling in the anchor cables and moving the ship ahead. The Americans spent a sleepless night kedging. By morning, they were well away from danger.

Slip-Ring Anchor

Slip-ring anchors are intended to eliminate the need for a trip line. The rode attaches to a ring, which is free to slide on the shank of the anchor. Under normal pull, the ring slides to the end of the shank and the flukes dig into the ground. If the boat reverses the pull on the rode, the ring slides down the shank to the crown of the anchor. Strain on the rode now pulls the anchor out backward.

Slip-ring anchors are popular with anglers who fish areas with rocky bottoms. They are also useful as lunch hooks. However, a slip-ring anchor should *never* be used as an overnight or permanent moorage hook. If the wind shifts, the anchor will be jerked out of the bottom. Once the ring slides to the crown end, the anchor may not be able to reset itself and rapid dragging will result.

5

DOCKING AND DOCK LINES

Given a choice, U.S. boat owners prefer docking at a marina to lying off on a mooring. Docking gives easy access to shore and comes with fringe benefits such as running water, electricity, and perhaps cable TV or telephone. It's no wonder that marinas have become the preferred nesting ground of the American yacht. As with anchoring and mooring, docking in a marina requires both rope and the knowledge of how to use it.

Water-level fluctuations must be considered when securing to a wharf or pier. Coastal tides are the biggest culprits, although seiche action (wind-driven fluctuations) on the Great Lakes can cause unexpected level changes. A boat tied tightly at high water will be found "hanging" from its lines when the water goes down. Or, if tied correctly at low water, the boat will be banging around almost uncontrolled when the level comes up because of its excessively long dock lines.

In the broadest sense there are two docking situations: permanent and temporary. A perma- nent situation is that of a marina where the vessel is left unattended for long periods of time. Each dock line is made up for a specific job and these lines are normally left in place when the boat is away. On the other hand, temporary situations are often encountered when cruising. They may involve tying up for only an hour or two for dinner, or for an overnight stay in a transient marina.

Table 5-1

Comparison of Dock Lines

PERMANENT DOCKING	TEMPORARY DOCKING
• Lines Made for Specific Job	• No Advance Preparation
• Lines Left on Pier	• Lines Carried on Boat
• Fenders Secondary Importance	• Fenders Critical
• Long-term Safety Critical	• Short-term Setup

DOCK LINE BASICS

Despite the obvious differences, both permanent and temporary situations require similar use of dock lines. Over the years, sailors have devised a standard pattern for naming the various lines, depending primarily upon the location where they attach to the boat.

BOW AND STERN LINES

These lines run forward and aft from the bow and stern respectively. They are often the only ones used to temporarily moor a small boat (under twenty feet). Their importance diminishes on larger boats that rely more upon spring lines. Bow and stern lines should be run well up and down the pier to minimize fore and aft motion of the vessel.

SPRING LINES

These run roughly fore and aft alongside the vessel. They prevent movement forward or aft, while allowing for minor fluctuations in water level.

Spring lines are more important on boats over twenty feet in length.

BREAST LINES

These go directly from the vessel to the pier, roughly at right angles to the keel. They prevent the boat from moving away from the pier. Breasts are most useful when loading either passengers or cargo, but are never left in place for extended periods because of extreme strain if the water level changes.

Attempting to call each line by its exact proper name can be confusing, especially during docking and undocking maneuvers. One way to avoid this confusion is to follow the U.S. Navy procedure of numbering lines starting with Number One in the bow and working aft. Add the identifiers *port* or *starboard* as required.

The navy and large commercial ships also use a standard system of orders from the bridge to line handlers. These formal commands are designed to prevent misunderstandings, which

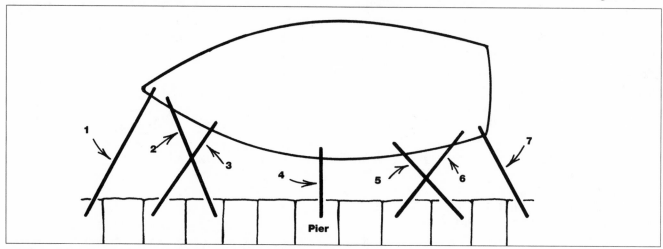

Each dock line has a specific name that indicates where it attaches on the boat and the direction it runs. From the bow, these lines are: 1. bow line; 2. after bow spring; 3. forward bow spring; 4. midships breast; 5. after quarter spring; 6. forward quarter spring; and 7. stern line. Note: Starboard lines are not shown; spring lines may land on the pier farther forward or aft than shown.

could prove deadly if a large ship's hawser parted unexpectedly. There's no requirement for formal commands on smaller vessels, where most line handling is done by the skipper's family. However, the skipper and crew should discuss each docking in advance to be sure everyone knows the plan. Also, the skipper must always speak loudly and clearly when passing orders to the crew.

Choice of Rope

Nylon is the overwhelming choice for dock lines because of its ability to stretch under load. Dock lines are relatively short, so any motion of the boat becomes a quick, sharp shock load on either the deck fitting or the bollard on the pier. Nylon stretches a bit to absorb some of this shock. This makes life aboard somewhat less jerky and reduces the possibility of damage to hardware. Three-strand twisted rope is easier to splice, although braided rope stands up better to chafe.

Dacron and polypropylene ropes both lack the stretch characteristics necessary in a dock line. In addition, poly rope has been known to chafe through in only a few minutes. This makes poly an especially poor choice for use on a vessel that will be unattended for extended periods. Natural-fiber manila or hemp rope may be used for dock lines, but care must be exercised to prevent rot and chafe.

Dock lines are fated for much shorter life spans than other pieces of cordage. This is especially true of those in permanent situations where the lines are constantly exposed to sunlight, saltwater, and chafe. Even the constant surging of the boat takes its toll. Since there is no practical way to measure the loss of strength in exposed dock lines, the only solution is to replace them at regular intervals. Vessels in northern climates may get two seasons out of a set of lines, while those docked down South may need new lines every six months or so.

Chafe was discussed in Chapter 2. The split-hose antichafe gear described there should be standard equipment on permanent dock lines. Boats are constantly in motion, even when

Commercial split-hose antichafe gear is installed on both bow lines of this sailboat. This owner knows the wisdom of providing chafe protection despite the well-designed Skene chocks on his boat.

docked in a quiet, well-protected harbor. This movement causes dock lines to constantly rub against chocks, fairleads, and other pieces of hardware. The amount of wear on any day is insignificant, but each day's damage is cumulative. Without chafe protection, a dock line can be worn through in less than a summer boating season.

PERMANENT DOCKING

The goal of a permanent setup is to hold the boat safely away from any pilings, piers, or catwalks during seasonal weather conditions. A perfect situation does not require the use of fenders to protect the hull, yet allows easy boarding from the pier. Such perfection is almost never accomplished because few docks allow the use of appropriate lines on both sides of the boat.

Permanent docking situations can be described by the number of attachment points for dock lines. A four-point situation gives shore-side attachment points on both sides of the boat, two at the bow and two at the stern. More common is a three-point situation that gives two attachment points at the stern (one on either side), but only one at the bow. The least desirable situation is *lying alongside*, in which all of the shoreside attachment points are on one side of the vessel.

For this discussion, attachment points are permanent fittings on piers or onshore. These should be cast steel cleats or substantial bollards, but wooden uprights and other structural parts of the pier are often pressed into service. Whenever possible, purpose-built mooring hardware should be used. Dock risers and other parts of the pier may not have the necessary strength to hold the boat in a blow. Worse, they may contain sharp edges that can chafe through the rope used for dock lines.

Making Up Dock Lines

Dock lines used in permanent situations are normally cut and spliced for the purpose. An eye splice is made in the boat end of the line. This eye is sized to fit the particular cleat on which it will be secured. The shore end does not receive an eye. Instead, it is deliberately left several feet long and the end is given a sailmaker's whipping. In service, the shore end of each line is adjusted until the boat is riding correctly in its dock. Adjustments to permanent dock lines are always made from the shore end so that their effect on the vessel can be immediately observed. Once the lines are correctly adjusted, docking becomes a matter of dropping each line over its appropriate cleat.

Snubbers and Mechanical Springs

The short length of dock lines means that shock loads occur every time the boat surges against them. Even the stretch of nylon does little to solve this problem, which can make spending time onboard uncomfortable. Several manufacturers produce rubber *snubbers* designed to cushion the shock of surging against a short dock line. Connecting eyes at either end of their heavy rubber band bodies allow insertion into a dock line.

Snubbers are not considered dependable enough to hold your boat without conventional rope

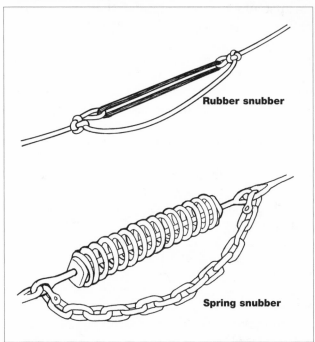

Rubber snubber

Spring snubber

Rubber snubbers are meant to absorb shock loads. While they are strong, snubbers have been known to fail. That's why there must be a bight of rope backing up the snubber to take over if it breaks.

Steel springs can also be used to take up shock loads in dock lines. Springs are necessary in all-chain setups, which have no stretch of their own. Springs may also be installed in rope dock lines as seen here.

backup. A bight of rope slightly longer than the fully stretched snubber should parallel it in the finished dock line. If the snubber should snap, the rope is standing by to keep your boat from drifting away.

Fiber rope portions of permanent dock tie-ups can be replaced by sections of chain containing mechanical springs. Chain provides maximum protection against chafe and avoids the risk of fiber rope snapping in unusually rough conditions. Since chain has no stretch, a mechanical spring is needed to soften shock loads. A slack length of safety chain around the spring allows full expansion and compression, yet maintains control of the boat should the mechanical spring break.

Chains in permanent dock tie-ups have snap hooks that clip to eyes bolted through the bow or stern of the boat. These hooks must be at least equal in strength to the chain and have positive-acting keepers to prevent them from slipping out of the eye if the chain becomes slack. Most often, chains are used to replace rope in the crossed stern lines of a three- or four-point situation. Care must be exercised when crossing chains because of the possibility that the mechanical springs might rub together and become entangled. If chains are crossed, the location of mechanical springs should be arranged so that they do not clash.

Dock Modifications

Engineers who design marina piers do their best to supply cleats, bollards, or other attachment points at logical locations. Unfortunately, what's logical for one boat may not be for another. A successful permanent tie-up often requires making minor modifications to create proper angles for spring lines or to place a dock riser where it will be most useful.

Additional cleats can be lag-bolted to wooden piers as needed. Dock cleats should be cast metal units designed for the purpose. If chains are to be used, eye bolts are required where they

connect to the pier. All hardware must be through-bolted with backing plates or washers and self-locking nuts. Piers and wharves belong to the marina. Management permission must be obtained before attempting any modifications. Drilling a hole in the wrong spot on a steel floating dock can leave you with a sinking feeling.

Aftermarket cast metal cleats like these can be added to wooden piers or wood decks on metal docks. Check with the marina management before installing.

It's convenient to leave permanent dock lines on the pier when you're out cruising. All too often, the lines are flung ashore or across catwalks where they lie waiting to trip the unwary. Line hangers eliminate this danger and make it easier to retrieve dock lines with a boat pole when returning. Hangers are easily bent from ¼-inch steel or aluminum bar stock available at hardware stores. Acceptable hangers also can be made of oak or other hardwood. The hanger needs to be only large enough to hold the eye in the end of the dock line.

Hangers should be placed where they can be conveniently reached from the boat, yet are not in a position to catch on the vessel as it leaves the dock. These requirements are often at odds with each other and a clever compromise may

Dock lines left behind while you're out cruising are always a problem. A simple hanger like this one holds them out of the water, yet swings out of the way for maneuvering the boat.

be necessary. One approach is to place the hanger at the end of a long swinging arm that can be rotated out of harm's way. Or the hanger may be attached to the back side of a piling.

FOUR-POINT SITUATION

A four-point situation occurs most often in marinas where boats are served by catwalks off a main central pier. For economy, each catwalk serves two vessels so that each boat slip has a

catwalk along only one side. The other side of the slip is delineated by an imaginary line drawn from the main pier to the piling at the outer end of the slip. This creates an oblong "box" of water in which the boat is docked. Attachment points occupy the corners of this box. In most cases attachment points on the pier are cleats, while those at the far end are the round pilings.

A minimum of four lines are used in a four-point situation, one from each quarter and two from the bow. Bow lines normally lead straight from the boat's mooring cleats to their respective pilings. Things aren't so simple in the stern. Here, the two lines cross: the port quarter line leads to a cleat on the right side of the dock, while the starboard line goes to the left side. Crossing stern lines accomplishes several things. It prevents the boat from moving sideways into either the catwalk or the neighboring vessel. And crossed lines are longer so they can accommodate fluctuations in water level.

When the dock space is significantly longer than the boat, the angle of the bow lines prevents the stern from coming back against the main pier.

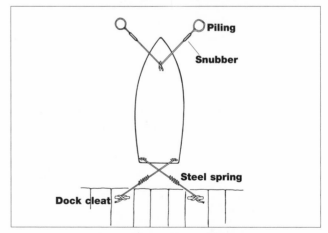

A four-point situation provides dock line attachment points at all four "corners." Crossing the stern lines helps center the boat in its dock space. Snubbers are used on the bow lines.

If this is not the case, however, two additional forward quarter springs are needed. Their length is set so that the stern can come close to the main pier—but not touch, even during heavy weather. A temporary breast line can be used to hold the boat against the catwalk for loading passengers.

A four-point situation can usually be arranged so that fenders are not needed. The "spring" action of the crossed stern lines should keep the boat in the center of its designated space. Another advantage of this arrangement is that the boat can be docked either bow or stern to the main pier. Powerboats are usually backed into their slips so that the cockpit is close to the pier. This allows for easy loading of passengers and gear as well as for socializing with people on the pier once the sun is below the yardarm.

Knots to Use

ON OFFSHORE PILINGS
An eye splice works best, but a bowline will get the job done. In either case, do your best work as either the splice or the knot will be out of arm's reach most of the time.

ON DOCK RINGS
Put a round turn through the ring and then take two half hitches. Or, for more security, try an anchor bend. An additional half hitch or two with either knot will put your mind at ease on stormy nights.

ON DOCK RISERS
Use risers only as a last resort, as most are only bolted in place and are subject to unexpected failure. A round turn and two half hitches works well as it can be quickly adjusted.

ON CLEATS
Take a full round turn around the cleat base and

two figure eights over the horns. Finish with a half hitch on both horns.

THREE-POINT SITUATION

A three-point situation eliminates one attachment point, usually the piling at the open end of the slip. This produces an L-shaped dock space that makes it virtually impossible to tie up the boat, so fenders are necessary. The side of the vessel against the catwalk will always need protection even when spring lines are rigged.

Whether the vessel is docked head-in or stern-in depends primarily on the location of its mooring and spring cleats. It may take considerable experimentation to discover the best heading for the boat and the best locations for the various lines. Typically, crossed stern lines perform the same function as in a four-point situation. They keep the

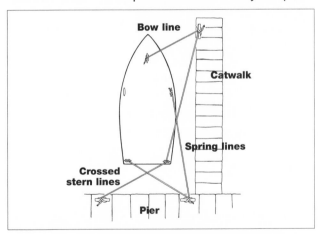

A three-point situation requires carefully balancing the pull of stern and spring lines. The boat will ride well away from the main pier, but may rub against the catwalk under some wind or current conditions.

stern centered in the dock space. Controlling the bow is a bit more difficult, as it involves balancing the pull of two or more spring lines.

If an after bow spring is rigged from a cleat about two thirds of the way forward on the boat, the stern can be pulled away from the catwalk. In the illustration, the pull of the starboard after bow spring is opposed by the port quarter stern line, which crosses to the right side of the dock.

A starboard forward quarter spring along the catwalk keeps the stern from moving back against the main pier. It also pulls the bow away from the catwalk. This line is opposed by the starboard quarter stern line, which crosses to the left side of the dock. The bow line controls how far the bow swings away from the catwalk.

Since all of these lines are under tension, they must be as long as possible to accommodate water-level fluctuations. Finally, a bow line should be rigged from the bow to the catwalk. Its only purpose is to check the swing of the bow away from the catwalk, so most of the time it should be slightly slack.

Because of the angle, the spring lines cannot keep the side of the vessel away from the catwalk at all times. Wind or current will easily push the hull against rough pilings or dock risers. Fenders must be rigged for protection. However, the three-point tie-up effectively prevents the boat from excessive motion forward or aft. This means that fendering is necessary only at major contact points.

Knots to Use

Use the same knots as in a four-point situation, except that all lines should be adjustable from their shore ends. It's normal to have to "play" the lines a bit from time to time to keep the boat riding where you want it. This is particularly true of the spring lines.

LYING ALONGSIDE

From a permanent docking standpoint, the worst possible situation is being forced to lie alongside a pier or wharf. Since it's impossible to push on a rope, none of the dock lines can be used to hold the vessel away from pilings or other rough surfaces. A surplus of properly located fenders is the only protection against scratched and gouged gel coat.

Spring lines do the bulk of the work when lying alongside. They hold the boat to the pier and prevent it from moving forward or backward. Bow and stern lines work to prevent their respective ends of the boat from swinging away from the pier. This is an important function since if the bow swings out, the stern must swing into the pier and damage is likely. In tidal waters it's common for after bow and forward quarter springs to cross each other near the vessel's midpoint. Extra length allows the spring lines to accommodate greater changes in the water level.

Adequate fendering is the best means of preventing hull damage. The most effective way of using fenders is to secure them on the vessel in the way of dock pilings or risers. Since they are attached

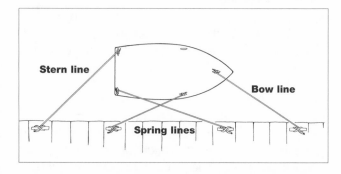

When a boat is lying alongside, it's impossible to keep it from rubbing on the pier. The spring, bow, and stern lines are used to maintain the boat's position along the pier, and fenders are used to protect the gel coat.

to the boat, the importance of properly set spring lines to fender performance can't be overstated. Movement of the vessel either forward or aft results in the fender being carried away from the dock riser, which is then free to begin chewing fiberglass. Good spring lines prevent excess motion and keep the fenders in position where they do the most good.

Tying alongside in areas that experience fluctuating water levels requires long spring lines. Longer lines have more play to accommodate level changes. Some people are reluctant to use long spring lines because of the widely held belief that lines should never cross lest the ropes chafe each other. While it's doubtful that two ropes would ever saw through each other, the suggestion not to cross spring lines may have some validity. The possibility of tangling exists any time two ropes come near one another. This is most likely to happen when departing if the lines are not removed in exactly the reverse order to which they were secured.

Knots to Use

Use the same knots as in a four-point situation, except that all lines must be adjustable from their shore ends. This situation requires frequent tending of the lines to keep the boat riding in the desired location.

TEMPORARY DOCKING

A quick visit to a waterfront restaurant and an overnight stay in a marina are examples of temporary docking situations. There is a tendency to look upon these situations as somewhat trivial. Lines are quickly thrown ashore in the rush to enjoy shoreside attractions. It's no wonder that improper temporary tie-ups are a major contributor to scratched gel coats and other topside damage.

Every boat should be equipped with a set of at least four lines dedicated to nothing except temporary docking. The two long lines should be equal in length to the vessel, while the two short lines should be at least half the length of the long ones. Thus, a thirty-two-foot cruiser needs at least two thirty-foot and two fifteen-foot lines. This is a *minimum* recommendation. Prudent skippers carry additional lines of up to twice the length of the boat to meet unexpected situations. All dock lines should have a large eye spliced in one end and a sailmaker's whipping on the other. Make the eye large enough to slip over dock pilings, risers, or bollards normally encountered in the vessel's cruising area.

In the reverse of a permanent situation, it's the spliced eye of a temporary dock line that is sent ashore. This allows adjusting its length from the deck of the boat. Anyone who has had to get up at 0300 hours to adjust dock lines knows the advantage of being able to do all the work from on board the vessel. Also, an eye in the shore end of a temporary line allows two or more vessels to share the same bollard by dipping the eye.

Securing the Lines

Temporary docking situations are identical to those involved in permanent docking: four- and

Dipping the Eye

Dock lines from two vessels can share the same bollard if both lines have large enough eyes. These can be either a spliced eye or just a large bight of line created by a bowline knot. The mooring line eye from one boat is dropped over top of the bollard in the usual manner. The second boat's eye is brought under and up through the eye of the first line before being dropped over the bollard. Either vessel can now cast off without disturbing the other. The first vessel simply lifts its eye off the bollard as usual. If the second boat gets away first, its eye is lifted over the bollard and allowed to drop back through the eye in the line of the first vessel.

three-point or alongside. Dock lines are secured in much the same manner. The major difference is that a lower degree of perfection is necessary because shoreside attachment points never seem to be in quite the right place. Modifying the pier isn't practical for a short stay, so lines are seldom run to best advantage. Fendering becomes critical to prevent hull damage.

It's common for boats that do extensive cruising

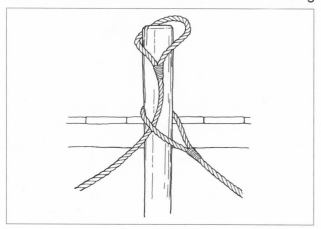

The process of *dipping the eye* allows two boats to secure to the same piling, yet either can leave without removing the other's lines. The eye of the first boat's line is looped over the piling in the normal fashion. The eye of the second boat's line is first pulled upward *through* the eye of the first boat's line. Then, the second eye is dropped over the piling.

to have additional spring cleats installed. These cleats allow greater freedom in setting up dock lines. Additional small cleats may also be installed to make the job of hanging fenders easier.

Knots to Use

ON OFFSHORE PILINGS
Tie a bowline to match the diameter of the piling. Do your best work as this knot will be out of arm's reach most of the time.

ON DOCK RINGS
Put a round turn through the ring and then take two half hitches. Or, for more security, try an anchor bend.

ON DOCK RISERS
Use risers only as a last resort, as most are only bolted in place and are subject to unexpected failure. A round turn and two half hitches works well, as it can be adjusted from shore.

ON CLEATS
Take a full round turn around the cleat base and two figure eights over the horns. Finish with a half hitch on one horn.

RIGGING EFFECTIVE FENDERS

Fenders are temporary devices intended to protect the hull against damage when docking. They are often incorrectly called "bumpers," a word that properly describes flimsy tin decorations on automobiles. Inflatable vinyl fenders are standard equipment on modern boats. The most common of these are cylindrical in shape with a vertical hole through the middle for an attachment line. Also available are cylinder-shaped fenders with eyes at either end for two lines. A style common in European waters and gaining popularity in the United States is a large, round, inflated fender. Soft vinyl and air pressure combine in all of these fenders to cushion the hull against damage.

Cylindrical fenders are popular because they can be hung either vertically or horizontally as required. The vertical position protects against smooth walls by rolling as the boat moves fore and aft. For protection from a piling or dock riser, horizontal positioning works best. Horizontal orientation allows the fender to "roll" up and down as the water level rises or falls.

No matter which orientation, fenders hanging from the boat provide better protection than those tied to the pier. Changes in water level are automatically accommodated by fenders on the vessel: they go up or down with the boat. But

These round Scandinavian-style fenders are well suited to protect a heavy trawler yacht. However, it would be better to suspend them from cleats rather than from a decorative wooden handrail.

those on the pier do not move up or down. Falling water can leave them hanging well above the boat, where they do little good except as a soft perch for seagulls.

MANEUVERING ON DOCK LINES

Maneuvering into or out of a small slip is never easy. It's a job made more difficult by strong winds or currents. This is especially true if the wind or current is at right angles to the pier instead of parallel to it. The sideways drift of a shallow-draft powerboat in high winds can sometimes exceed its forward motion. Judicious use of

dock lines may be the only way to control the boat's movements under these conditions.

Safety Warning

Any discussion of maneuvering with dock lines must begin with a word of warning. These procedures are not without their dangers. A rope pulled through an unsuspecting hand can leave nasty burns behind. A careless moment can result in injuries to hands, fingers, legs, and toes. Young children should be kept well away from any rope that is under tension or is likely to come under strain suddenly. The crew should be experienced in line handling and the entire operation should be planned in advance.

Heaving a Line

Many times the only way to get a line from the boat to shore is by heaving. Large ships carry special light ropes called *heaving lines* just for this purpose. On pleasure boats the size of the line being sent ashore seldom exceeds one inch in diameter. Lines up to this size are easy enough to throw, so you shouldn't need a special heaving line. It's possible to heave ropes as small as $3/8$-inch diameter. Smaller rope does not have enough mass to carry well, especially in high winds.

True heaving lines have a weighted end called a *monkey's fist.* A small amount of weight helps get maximum distance, but raises certain dangers. The person doing the catching can be injured or knocked out by a weight on the end of the incoming line. An unweighted line can be heaved quite satisfactorily and is much less dangerous.

The following instructions apply to a right-hander. (Sorry lefties, you'll have to reverse things.) Coil the line loosely into your left hand. Make coils as large as you find comfortable to hold. When the entire rope is coiled, take one third to one half of the loops into your right

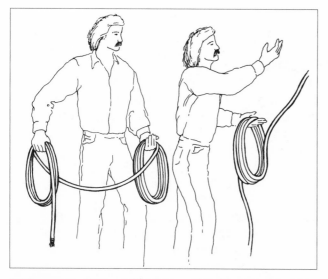

It takes practice to accurately heave a line. The bulk of the line is coiled in the left hand while the right hand holds only a few coils. Enough slack is allowed between the hands for free arm movement. The actual cast is a somewhat sidearm "round-house" movement much like that of an Olympic discus thrower.

hand. Leave at least an arm span of uncoiled rope between your hands. Stand with your left shoulder favored toward the target.

Keep your eye on the target. Swing your right arm to get a "feel" of the rope and to gauge the throw. The actual toss is made with a big "round-house" motion of the entire right arm. Let go of the loops in your right hand just before it points at the target. (A proper heaving motion is very similar to that used by a discus thrower in the Olympics.) The weight of the loops thrown by the right hand should begin to pull additional rope off your open left hand, which should now be pointing at the target. Let the rope take as many loops off your left hand as possible. A good toss should put the line right across the shoulder of the catcher onshore.

Beware the bitter end when heaving a line. More than one enthusiastic sailor has heaved the entire coil, leaving him with nothing to secure to his boat.

The bitter end is best secured to a deck cleat. Or, have an assistant keep a two-fisted grip on the bitter end during the heaving. If you're alone, it may be possible to hold the bitter end between the thumb and forefinger of your left hand. Standing on the bitter end with one foot is another (and obviously dangerous) way of preventing the entire coil from "going by the board."

Surging a Line

Another useful technique is known as *surging the line*. This is done whenever the pull on a line exceeds what a crew member can handle unassisted. The average person should be surging the line whenever the pull exceeds fifty pounds. Surging works on the principle that friction and resistance to motion are created any time a rope is bent at nearly right angles around a fixed object. This friction reduces the pull on the bitter end to an amount that most people can handle.

Surging is normally done under one horn of a cleat, although almost any fixed object will work. Simply lead the line under one horn and then bring the bitter end almost straight up. The horn is now caught in a nearly right-angle bend in the rope. An ordinary person can create enough friction by surging the line this way to hold several hundred pounds of load. A surged line can be paid out smoothly by easing the tension on the bitter end.

Looping the Piling

Many times there is nobody onshore to release a line used to maneuver away from a dock. Since it's impractical to have someone swim back to shore to retrieve this line, the best solution is to plan ahead and "loop" the piling or bollard. Take the line from a cleat on the boat to shore and around the piling. Bring the bitter end back on board, creating a large loop. A crew member surges the bitter end during maneuvers and releases it on command. The loop around the piling disappears and the rope comes free from shore. It is hauled back on board with care to be sure that the line does not sink and become entangled in a propeller. Also, someone should be standing by with a knife to cut the line should it become tangled ashore.

Winding Ship

The process of turning a vessel end-for-end is known as *winding ship*. The term goes back to the days of sailing vessels prior to steam tugboats. Ships that sailed into port had to be turned around before they could sail back out. This was often done in a specially created area known as a *winding basin*. Ropes would be rigged to pull the stern away from the wharf by brute force of men or animals. God's good wind would then be allowed to catch the ship and provide the motive power for completing the turn. Using wind to power this maneuver is the origin of the name.

To "wind" a boat, cast off all lines except an after bow spring as shown in the illustration. Push the stern out and allow the wind to pivot the hull through position A until the bow is pointed directly at the pier. At this point, position B, what started as the spring line has become a bow line. Allow the boat to continue pivoting through position C while a forward quarter spring is heaved ashore. Use this second line to pull the boat parallel to the pier. Depending upon the speed and direction of the wind, it is almost always necessary to protect the bow with several fenders. A crew member should be standing by to place them as needed.

Wind is not the only motive power that can accomplish this maneuver. River current can also be used to great effect.

Walking Along Shore

From time to time it's necessary to move an unmanned vessel along a length of pier or parallel

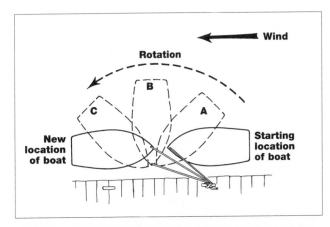

Winding allows a boat to be turned end-for-end without untying it from the pier. All lines are cast off except an after bow spring. The boat moves forward and then pivots to position A under pressure of the wind. At position B, the bow will need fendering against the pier. A stern line is cast ashore when the boat reaches C.

to shore. This can be done quite effectively with two lines: a bow breast and a forward quarter spring. Before attempting to move the vessel, be sure the helm is amidships or turned slightly *away* from shore. All of the pulling force moving the boat is exerted on the spring line. This not only moves the boat forward but pulls the stern toward the pier while the bow is kicked away. Keeping a short stay on the breast line checks the twisting motion and the boat moves parallel to the pier. Slacking the breast line allows the bow to pivot out and the vessel will gain distance away from the pier.

Entering a Confined Dock

Many vessels are docked in spaces scarcely larger than their hulls. Wind conditions can require that considerable way be kept on while entering the slip to maintain steerage. This leaves precious little space to stop the boat before the nose crunches against the pier. One solution is to rig a spring line from the outer corner of the dock space. At the boat end, this line should have an eye made specifically to fit a cleat mounted approximately amidships. The other end should have an eye large enough to slip over a dock piling.

Upon entering the dock, a crew member secures this line to the midships cleat. Bursts of reverse thrust are used as the vessel enters the dock to check headway and allow your crew member more time to drop his or her line over the appropriate piling or dock riser. This is accomplished when the boat is at position A in the illustration. Once the line is secure, it does the work of stopping the boat. Motor forward at dead idle with the rudder turned slightly *away* from the spring line to keep the vessel centered in the dock

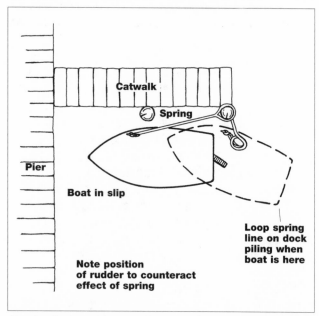

A spring line greatly assists docking. Attach it forward of amidships and loop it over a piling when the boat is at position A. The spring must be long enough to allow the boat to fully enter the dock before coming taut. Motor at dead slow on the spring with the rudder turned slightly *away* from the dock to hold position while the remaining dock lines are secured.

while the other dock lines are secured.

Using a spring line in this manner will cause the vessel to come hard against one pier. Using plenty of fenders can prevent damage. For convenience, these fenders can be attached to the pier. As mentioned earlier, however, fenders hung from the boat are usually more effective.

Clearing a Dock #1:
Current/Wind from Ahead

The goal is to let the wind catch the bow and pivot it away from the pier. Cast off all lines except a forward quarter spring. This allows the bow to swing away from the pier. It also allows the stern to swing in, so have fenders rigged. Going ahead at dead idle speed may help to keep the stern off the pier as long as it does not prevent the bow from swinging. When the bow is pointed well away from the pier, slip the spring line and go ahead at harbor speed.

Clearing a Dock #2:
Current/Wind from Astern

This is the same basic procedure as #1 above, except that the stern is allowed to pivot out on an after bow spring. Once the stern is clear, release the spring line and back away from the pier into clear water.

Clearing a Dock #3:
Being Set On

Attempting to depart is difficult if the wind (or current) is setting the boat against a pier. One solution is to run a line from as far forward on the vessel to a point well onshore. The shore attachment should be somewhat aft of the bow, but not as much as a spring line. Back down on this line with the rudder turned *away* from the pier. The vessel will move backward to A in the illustration below. Backward motion ceases when this line takes full tension. At that point, the boat will begin to pivot around its bow through position B. The stern naturally swings away from the pier. Slip the line ashore at C when the stern is clear of all obstructions. Back into open water before resuming forward motion.

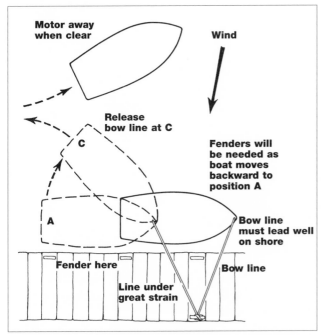

This technique allows departure while being set on the pier by wind or current. Release all lines except a bow line sent well ashore as shown. Back down slowly, allowing the boat to move to position A where all further movement aft is prevented by the line. The boat will now swing through B to position C. Fenders will be needed to protect the bow. At position C release the line and back clear of the pier.

Clearing a Pier #4: Being Set On

Protect the bow well with fenders. Release all lines except an after bow spring, which should be run to a point on the pier as far aft along the vessel as possible. This spring *must* come from the absolute point of the bow. Motor ahead at dead

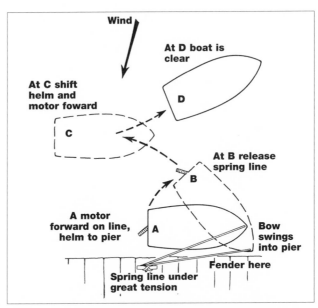

Another way to depart while being set upon the pier by wind or current is with an after bow spring. This line must lead from as close to the centerline at the bow as possible. Motor ahead with the rudder turned *toward* the pier to position B. Release the line and back away to position C before going ahead.

slow with the helm hard over toward the pier. The bow will pivot against the pier on the fenders. This is position B in the illustration above. Release the spring and reverse away from the dock. (Note: If the spring line is not led from as far forward on the boat as possible, the bow will not pivot properly and this maneuver will fail.)

Turning While Departing a Pier

A forward quarter spring can assist in backing out of a narrow slip, especially in a crosswind. Rig this spring so it is slack at position A in the illustration on page 98, but becomes taut at B just after the pivot point of the vessel clears the pier. Release all other lines and back down with the helm toward the side on which the spring is set. The combination of the spring line and the rudder pivots the boat around starting at position B. Careful fendering is necessary when the side of the boat comes into contact with the corner of the pier. Release the spring at C in the illustration and motor ahead once the boat is shaped up in the main channel.

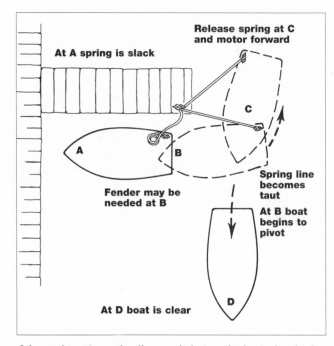

A forward quarter spring line can help turn the boat when backing out of a dock. The line is slack at A when the boat is lying in its berth. It becomes taut as the boat backs to position B. The spring helps pivot the boat to position C, where it can be released to allow the boat to motor away.

6

SPECIAL SITUATIONS

The need to "know the ropes" aboard modern boats goes far beyond anchoring, mooring, and docking. Other tasks include towing a dinghy or water-skier, locking through a canal, or possibly towing another vessel in an emergency. Each of these situations requires picking the right rope for the job and putting it to proper use.

STREAMING A SEA ANCHOR

By tradition, sea anchors are usually discussed as part of heavy-weather seamanship. The use of sea anchors (or drogues) is considered the best method of keeping a small vessel's bow into the wind and waves during gale or hurricane conditions. Another, seldom mentioned, function of a sea anchor emerges during emergency breakdowns offshore. Few boats carry enough rode to properly anchor to the bottom at any distance offshore. They can't anchor should a mechanical breakdown occur.

Anyone who has participated in search-and-rescue at sea knows that it is far more difficult to find a drifting boat than one that stays put. Streaming a sea anchor keeps a disabled boat close to its last reported position. A boat riding to a sea anchor is much easier for the Coast Guard or a commercial assistance towboat to locate.

While they are of great value in surviving emergencies, sea anchors often perform more mundane tasks. Small versions are found aboard sport fishing boats. Streaming a drogue allows anglers to slow their drift across a productive school of fish. Slowing the drift allows more time to catch fish. Sea anchors for surviving an ocean storm or holding position while awaiting rescue are considerably larger and more robust than those used in fishing. Otherwise, the details of construction and the methods of employment are quite similar.

Sea Anchor Design

The traditional sea anchor is a canvas cone kept open at both ends by wire rings. A bridle or yoke at the wide opening allows attachment of the rode through a swivel. The anchor is deployed

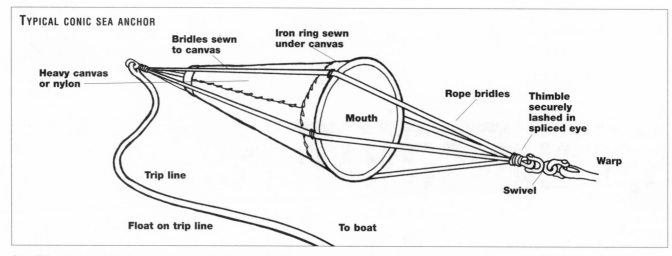

TYPICAL CONIC SEA ANCHOR

Bridles sewn to canvas

Iron ring sewn under canvas

Heavy canvas or nylon

Rope bridles

Thimble securely lashed in spliced eye

Mouth

Warp

Trip line

Swivel

Float on trip line

To boat

A traditional sea anchor is a canvas cone held open at both ends by metal rings. The pointed end is not closed, but open enough to allow a small amount of water to flow through. The swivel between the rode and the sea anchor bridle prevents rotation of the drogue from causing hockles in the rope.

with the large opening toward the boat. A great deal of water is "caught" by the large end, but only a small amount can flow through the restricted small end. This small flow of water is needed to keep the drogue properly streamed and to cushion shock loads on the rode.

Modern sea anchors borrow ideas from aircraft parachutes. In fact, they look much like parachutes except that much of the canopy has been cut away. Some parachute-style sea anchors are mostly nylon webbing with plenty of holes between webs for water to flow. Others have a full canopy, but a large central vent. As with the canvas cone, the flow of water is necessary to keep the sea anchor properly deployed and to cushion shock loads.

The rode of either type should be equipped with a swivel to prevent hockles in the rope caused by rotation of the drogue. In addition, both types should be equipped with a trip line for retrieval. The trip line allows the drogue to

be pulled backward to the boat. This takes considerably less effort than trying to pull the boat up to the sea anchor by hauling in the rode.

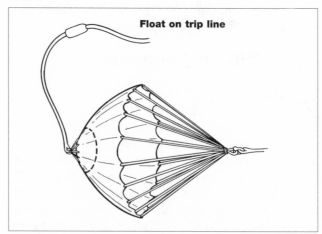

Float on trip line

A parachute-style sea anchor looks much like its aerial cousins. In fact, this type of drogue was developed from aircraft parachutes. The canopy may be solid but is more often vented to allow the flow of water.

The Sea Anchor Rode

Some authorities suggest using polypropylene rope for both the rode and the trip line. The reason is obvious: this type of cordage floats. Their argument is that floating rope gives better control and is less likely to tangle than line that does not float. Few pleasure boats have the storage space for carrying a dedicated sea anchor rode. So it's comforting that nylon, Dacron, and even manila rope have all been used successfully.

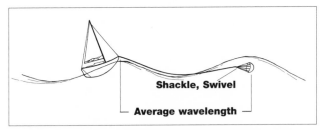

A sea anchor should be streamed ahead of the boat so that it is in the same part of its wave as the boat. If the boat is on the "uphill" side, that's where the drogue should be also. The sea anchor can be several waves ahead of the boat.

As with a bottom anchor, the length of the rode has considerable impact on a sea anchor's performance. The standard advice is to let out enough rode so that the boat and the sea anchor are "in step" on the waves. This means that if the boat is on the crest of its wave, the drogue should be on a crest of its own. As with other aspects of seamanship, there are no absolute instructions. The rode will have to be "played" to discover the best length for the sea conditions.

Emergency Sea Anchors

Rigging an emergency sea anchor is an exercise in creativity. Just about anything you can name has been used. The only criteria are that it have a relatively large cross-section to create drag through the water and that it have an attachment point for a rope. Stout metal buckets are an excellent substitute for a commercial drogue. Don't try it with a plastic bucket, however; the handle will pull out of the plastic. Outboard craft have successfully used portable six-gallon fuel tanks as jury sea anchors.

Another possibility is to pay out your regular anchor rode *on the bight*. That is, tie both ends of the rode to the bow of the boat and let the middle stream forward in a big loop. Rope dragging through the water creates a surprising amount of resistance. A variation of this technique can be used to hold the vessel's bow at an angle to the waves. Secure one end of the bight to the bow and the other to a cleat on the side of the vessel somewhat forward of amidships. The vessel should lie at an angle with that side slightly to the waves. Adjusting the attachment point will change the angle of the boat.

TOWING A DINGHY

Hard Dinghy

Few boats are as much fun to own as a saucy whitehall or peapod rowing dinghy. Not only are they beautiful to look at, but rowing is a healthful way to explore quiet backwaters or to go ashore from an anchorage. Towing a hard dinghy is far less problem than most people envision. Success starts with the dinghy. It should have a pronounced exterior keel ending in a skeg to promote good tracking. Flat-bottomed boats with little or no keel tend to skitter around under tow. The towing eye should be located well down the stem near the waterline. This ensures that the pull of the painter (tow line) lifts the bow slightly and forces the skeg at the stern deeper into the water for better tracking.

A properly designed hard dinghy tows with surprisingly little resistance behind sailboats and powerboats at displacement speeds. Hard dinghies are no longer towed behind high-speed, planing hull powerboats. The speed of the big boat far exceeds the hull speed of the dinghy, which is not intended to plane.

Back in the 1920s (when a lack of public marinas made towing a dinghy almost mandatory), they had a way to tow a dinghy at planing speeds. The painter would be adjusted until the small boat was riding on the front edge of the wake "table" behind the big boat. In this location the dinghy would be constantly "falling" forward, off the table at a speed equal to the cruiser. This technique takes a bit of practice to learn—not to mention the willingness to risk a perfectly good dinghy.

Double-braid nylon rope is suggested for the dinghy tow line (properly, the painter). It has a bit less stretch than twisted rope but greater resistance to chafe. Dacron braid has little or no ability to cushion shock loads because of its low stretch. Both nylon and Dacron have one major disadvantage: they sink. Many's the boat that's wrapped its dinghy painter around a propeller. This accident takes place while docking after a long run. The boat is slowed and the dinghy overtakes it, allowing the painter to sink into harm's way.

Polypropylene rope does float, and thus avoids the danger of getting wrapped in a propeller. However, poly rope has little stretch to cushion shock loads. An even worse characteristic is its slipperiness, which allows knots to untie themselves and splices to pull apart. A successful dinghy painter can be made out of poly rope, but all eye splices should have extra tucks. Regular checks must be made to be sure the rope doesn't untie itself from the cleat on the big boat.

Most people tow on painters that are entirely too short. A thirty-foot line is not out of order to tow a nine-foot boat. Some experts suggest painters of seventy-five to one hundred feet, especially on open water in rough weather. Seasoned sailors often carry two painters: a short

one for daysailing or motoring in congested waters; and a long one for offshore passages.

No matter what the length, the painter should be either spliced directly to the dinghy's towing eye or attached with an oversize shackle. A shackle allows changing painters, but invites disaster if the pin pulls out unexpectedly. Whether spliced to the towing eye or not, the eye splice in the dinghy end of the painter must be protected with a solid nylon or metal thimble.

Inflatable Dinghy

At low speeds, inflatables can be towed in much the same manner as hard dinghies. However, the large wet surface created by their relatively flat, wide bottoms makes towing inflatables inefficient at speeds over dead slow. Their drag retards the speeds of sailboats excessively. At planing speeds, this drag becomes sufficient to snap the painter or rip the towing eye off the bow of the inflatable. Adjusting the length of the tow line does not improve the situation to any great degree.

Reducing wet surface is the only way to make towing an inflatable dinghy easier. This can be done by raising the bow out of the water and tying it to the center of the big boat's taffrail. Only the stern ends of the flotation tubes remain in the water. The outboard motor should be removed from the boat when towing in this manner. If the outboard remains installed on the transom of the inflatable, it is likely to be swamped with seawater.

EMERGENCY TOWING

Sooner or later, everyone gets involved in towing a disabled boat. While the majority of these "good Samaritan" tows are successful, taking another vessel in tow is not something to be treated lightly. Towing involves elements of risk. These risks escalate dramatically as the weather deteriorates and wave heights build. Leave salvage towing to the professionals who have the equipment and the experience to get the job done.

Risks of Towing

No one can foresee every possible danger involved in towing. However, the more common dangers include:

ROPE INJURIES

Trying to hold a tow line in your hands as it comes under strain can result in severe rope burns. Even cleating a rope under strain can be dangerous if a finger gets caught in a bight of rope on the bitt. The whipping action of a rope that breaks can cause serious injuries.

HARDWARE FAILURE

Deck hardware on contemporary pleasure boats is not made for the rigors of towing. Cleats can break and send pieces of metal flying with lethal force. Or an improperly mounted cleat may pull off the deck with similar results. (Hardware failure is so common that U.S. Coast Guard and commercial towboats have special metal shields to protect their crews.)

LOSS OF CONTROL

Pleasure boats are not designed to tow and do not have towing bits properly located on their centerlines. The strain of a tow on a stern quarter cleat causes the towing boat to lose much of its maneuverability. This has severe consequences when entering harbors or crossing bars in rough weather.

TRIPPING

Tripping is professional tugboat jargon for a tug being rolled over by its tow. This happens when the tow line pulls at right angles to the keel of the

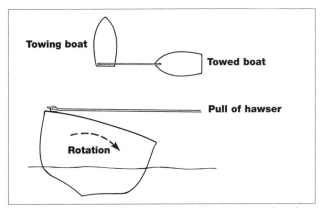

A towing boat can be tripped by its tow. This happens when the hawser is at nearly right angles to the keel. Pull on the hawser rotates the boat as shown and may cause it to capsize.

towing vessel, as shown in the drawing. A vessel that is tripped by its tow rolls over surprisingly fast. It is not uncommon for everyone on the tripped boat to be trapped and killed.

PROP WRAP

During the hectic moments of setting up a tow it's easy for the tow line to sink unnoticed. This allows it to become wrapped around the towing boat's propeller and shaft. The inevitable result is two disabled boats instead of one.

Federal Rules of the Road require all vessels to render assistance to others in peril of being lost at sea. However, there is an important modifier in this requirement that you should never overlook. The law does not require you to put yourself, your boat, or your passengers in danger to rescue another vessel. Towing with a pleasure boat not designed specifically for the job is dangerous work. As a private boat operator, you can't be forced to take another vessel in tow. More important, you should never undertake a tow if you have the slightest doubt of a successful outcome.

The crew of the towing boat should consist of at least two experienced persons. The skipper stays at the helm at all times and is in charge of the operation. The deckhand is responsible for handling all lines, especially the tow rope. In addition, the deckhand must keep the skipper informed of events involved in setting up the tow. This is particularly true if the skipper's view astern is obscured from the helm station.

All persons on board both boats should put on life preservers, even in calm water. It is possible for the strains involved in towing to cause a boat to roll over unexpectedly (see Tripping). The vessel being towed should hoist its distress flag to alert other vessels of the situation. At night, the towing vessel may illuminate the tow line and towed boat with a spotlight to serve the same purpose. The nearest Coast Guard station should be notified of the tow and its intended destination. This notification sets the stage for an official search-and-rescue mission, should it become necessary. Once both vessels have reached safe harbor, the Coast Guard should again be notified that everyone is safe.

Three Types of Towing

Most people think that towing means pulling another vessel at the end of a long rope. This is only one of the three forms of towing used on the water and recognized in the Rules of the Road. The three forms are:

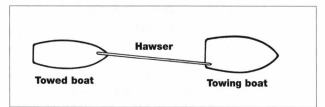

Towing astern with a hawser is the most common method for pleasure boats. As few cruisers are equipped with a towing bitt, the hawser must go to a quarter cleat as shown. This creates maneuvering difficulties.

1. Towing Astern—This is the conventional method of towing using a line from the stern of the towboat to the bow of the disabled boat. Towing astern is the method of choice when two pleasure boats are involved.

2. Towing Alongside—In this method the towing vessel is tied alongside the incapacitated boat (*on the hip*). Towing alongside offers greater control in crowded waters or when docking, but requires a high degree of skill. Substantial fenders are needed to prevent damage to both boats.

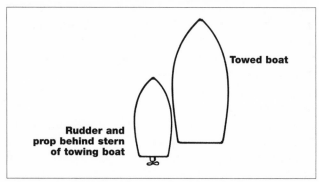

Towing alongside takes expert crew work and a lot of fenders, but it may provide more control of the tow in crowded harbors. It should never be attempted with any sea running.

3. Pushing Ahead—This method is almost never done with pleasure boats as they are not properly equipped for this maneuver. Pushing ahead is popular with commercial barge tow operators on the Mississippi River and its tributaries.

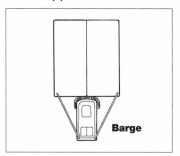

Pushing ahead is the third way to tow. This is common with barges on the Mississippi River system, but is seldom done by pleasure craft.

Towing Hawsers

In the tugboat trade, the rope used to tow astern is known as a *hawser*, no matter how big or small it may be. Large oceangoing tugboats often use steel wire hawsers thousands of feet long. In the pleasure-boat world, wire towing hawsers are unknown and hawsers are made of synthetic fiber rope. Choosing the correct fiber and construction for the hawser is critical.

NYLON ROPE

The ability to stretch is nylon's major advantage in towing because it cushions shock loads that occur from time to time. However, stretch is also nylon's major drawback. Small-diameter nylon rope may stretch to the point where physical damage is done to the individual fibers. Or if a piece of deck hardware breaks loose, a taut nylon rope will send it flying like a shot from a catapult. Reduced stretch and chafe resistance are the reasons that double-braid nylon rope is considered superior to three-strand twisted rope for towing.

POLYPROPYLENE ROPE

Poly rope has the decided advantage of floating. However, it also has almost no ability to stretch. Shock loads are transmitted undiminished to deck cleats on both the towing boat and the disabled vessel. Another drawback is poly's susceptibility to chafe. These drawbacks limit poly line to dinghy painters and other uses where the loads are relatively small and a rope with positive buoyancy is an advantage.

DACRON ROPE

Dacron rope also has virtually no stretch but is less susceptible to chafe than poly rope. Commercial towing companies often use braided Dacron rope for its strength and ease of handling.

TOWING ASTERN

Simple Towing Astern

A simple situation might involve giving a tow to another boat that's out of fuel. If the towing vessel is larger than the disabled craft and the weather is fair, all that's necessary is to connect a tow line between them. An anchor rode from the towed vessel makes an excellent emergency tow line. It should be sufficiently strong for the purpose and long enough to allow adjusting the length of the tow as needed.

Disconnecting the anchor and chain from the rope is suggested, but not always necessary in calm conditions. In rough weather or if the tow is expected to last for an extended period, however, the anchor and chain should be unshackled from the rope. Secure the anchor end of the rope to a bitt on the foredeck of the disabled vessel and send the rest over to the towing boat. Extra tow line is best kept aboard the towing boat since that boat does all of the maneuvering.

The vessel being towed tracks best if the tow line leads directly off its bow on the centerline. If the boat has an anchor roller, lead the tow line through it. Otherwise, lead the line through a chock or fairlead placed as close to the centerline of the disabled vessel as possible. On trailerable craft the tow line should be attached to the bow eye to ensure that the strain is on the boat's centerline. Using the bow eye also pulls the towed boat up and over the waves instead of down and into the water.

On the towing vessel it is often necessary to secure the hawser to a stern quarter cleat because few pleasure boats are built with a centerline towing bitt. This results in an eccentric drag—more pull from the tow on one side of the boat than on the other. Steering becomes difficult and maneuvering safely in close quarters is often impossible. The towing boat tends to turn toward the side on which the line is cleated. (If the line is cleated on the port side, the boat will tend to circle left.) "Crabbing" is usually acceptable on tows of short duration or distance, but can prove difficult or dangerous in heavy weather.

Even in simple situations, the tow line should never be attached to just one bitt on either the disabled boat or the towing boat. *Always* carry the bitter end to a second bitt or other substantial portion of the vessel where it is double-secured. This ensures that if the primary bitt should break or pull loose, parts will not be catapulted off the boat. The second attachment point is not intended to allow the tow to continue, just to prevent serious injuries to the crew of either boat. Even with this protection, never allow anyone to sit or stand in the direct "line of fire," should the tow rope break or a bitt pull loose.

Also, both boats should have someone standing by with a knife or small ax to cut the hawser in an emergency. Cutting a hawser under strain is always dangerous. The recoiling rope can cause injuries. However, there are times when cutting away the tow is the only way to protect the safety of both boats.

Complex Towing Astern

On a longer tow, or in foul weather, the biggest problem is often the seemingly simple task of attaching the tow line to the towboat. As noted, an off-center tow line results in handling and maneuvering problems for the towing boat. In rough water the towing vessel may not be able to afford any loss of control.

A towing bridle can be improvised to put the strain of the tow line on the centerline and improve the maneuverability of the towing vessel. The simplest bridle is just a short length of line equal in strength to the tow line. The bridle line has a small eye spliced in one end and is attached to one quarter bitt at the other. Feed the tow line through the bridle eye before attaching it to the bitt on the opposite quarter. When strain comes on the tow line, the bridle eye pulls it to the centerline of the towing boat.

This improvised bridle centers the strain of the tow, but the towing boat will still be severely hampered in maneuverability because the pull from the tow is coming onto the tow boat *behind* its propeller and rudder. Strain from the tow prevents the stern from pivoting properly during turns and other maneuvers. This must be kept in mind, especially when choosing a safe harbor.

Well offshore, a long tow line generally per-

Passing a Tow Line in Rough Seas

Attempting to heave a line from one boat to another in rough seas can be all but impossible. The person making the toss must hit a small moving target from the wet, slippery deck of another moving object. There's a much easier way to pass the tow line. Simply tie the tow line to an inflatable boat fender and let it drift downwind from the disabled boat. The towboat uses a hook to fish the fender out. With the fender comes the tow line.

forms better than a short one for several reasons. It allows the two boats to operate without fear of bumping into each other. Another reason is that a long hawser allows a substantial catenary to develop. As with an anchor rode, the catenary sag in a tow line has a shock-absorbing effect. Finally, a long line gives room for several waves between the two boats.

The length of the tow line should be adjusted so that both boats are on corresponding faces of different waves. That is, if the tow boat is climbing up the back of a wave, the disabled vessel should also be going "uphill" on its own wave. This is known as *towing in step*, or *synchronous towing*. Keeping the vessels in step helps avoid unnecessary jerks on the tow line

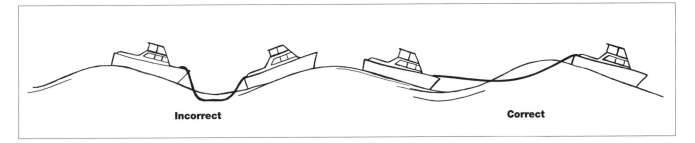

Incorrect   Correct

The hawser should be adjusted so the boats are "in step." This means that both should be on the same face of their respective waves. If they are out of step, one will be rushing ahead under pressure from a following sea while the other is being slowed by climbing up the wave ahead. This leads to jerks and strains on the hawser. If the boats are close together, it can result in the tow hitting the towing boat.

that would occur if they were on opposite sides of their waves.

Preventing Yawing

Yawing is the motion of a vessel's bow to the left or right of its intended track. Some boats under tow will yaw in only one direction, say to port. This is unusual. It's far more common for a boat that is being towed to yaw back and forth—port to starboard—as it is pulled through the water. While there is no absolute cure for yawing, some techniques have proven useful.

MOVING WEIGHT AFT

Redistributing the load aboard the vessel being towed will often result in a dramatic decrease in yawing, especially when towing a dinghy or other small boat. The vessel under tow usually tracks best if the bow is slightly high and the stern slightly low. (This is particularly true of small, light powerboats.)

A BRIDLE ON THE TOW

A bridle reduces yawing if it is properly constructed. Both legs of the bridle must be exactly the same length. The point where the bridle legs join the towing hawser requires special attention to reduce the inevitable chafe and wear. Bridle

legs are usually secured to bitts on the foredeck of the vessel under tow.

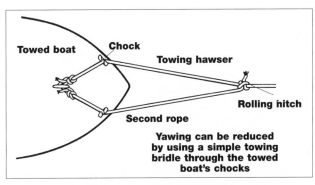

A bridle on the towed boat will help reduce yawing. A second rope is secured to the hawser with a rolling hitch. Both this rope and the hawser are adjusted until the tow rides smoothly.

When a vessel under tow yaws to port (left), the starboard (right) leg of the bridle takes all of the strain while the port (left) leg goes lazy. Pull on the starboard side of the boat being towed tends to create a yawing motion in the opposite direction and the vessel comes back on course.

VEERING MORE HAWSER

This reduces the impact of the tow's yawing motion on the maneuverability of the towing vessel. A longer hawser also drags deeper in the water. This drag inhibits the bow of the towed vessel from slewing off course.

ADJUSTING SPEED
Slowing down is often the most effective means of controlling yawing. High speed exaggerates all handling problems, so it's little wonder that yawing of the tow is more pronounced at higher speeds. Reducing speed is a proven method of reducing yawing.

No action of the towing boat will completely eliminate yawing of the tow. The goal is to minimize yawing to an amount that allows for safe maneuvering of the towing vessel.

Making Port
A long tow line makes sense at sea, but can lead to difficulties when you are entering crowded harbors. Other skippers won't be expecting a long rope between two boats—even if one of them is flying a distress signal. Crossing a rough bar may require keeping the tow line extended, but it should be shortened as soon as possible after reaching calm water.

Often, just slowing down to normal "no wake" speed in the harbor will provide enough slack to allow for shortening the hawser. Don't shorten too much, however. A minimum distance between the vessels is needed to allow the towing vessel to slow or stop without being overrun by the disabled boat. Three or four boat lengths may be enough for a small, light boat. Larger, heavier boats have more momentum and are more of a threat to the towing vessel.

Ending the Tow
Extreme caution is needed when slowing down after reaching the destination. If the tow vessel slows too quickly, the disabled boat will override it and a serious collision is likely. Reduce speed slowly, starting well away from the final destination. As the rope goes slack, the towing vessel takes in excess hawser to prevent it from sinking and possibly becoming tangled in the propeller.

The hawser can be released at either end when the tow is broken, but for obvious reasons the owner of the line normally holds fast. It doesn't matter if the owner of the line is the person being towed or the skipper of the towing vessel.

Watch Engine Gauges When Towing

Towing requires the engine of your boat to work much harder than normal cruising does. This extra work can strain the engine's cooling and lubrication systems. Keep a sharp eye on the temperature and oil pressure gauges while towing to prevent engine damage. Coolant temperature is particularly critical. Cease towing if any gauge readings go out of the range specified by the engine manufacturer.

TOWING ON THE HIP

Commercial tugboat crews usually switch from towing astern to towing on the hip when entering a crowded harbor. Lashing their tugboat to the barge gives better control of both. In theory this technique should work just as well with pleasure boats. However, there are several safety issues that must be considered before attempting to tow on the hip:

- Crew Skill—Be realistic in assessing the experience of both crews in handling lines, rigging fenders, and handling boats. Towing on the hip should not be attempted by inexperienced crews.

- Boat Construction—Considerable strain can be expected on bitts or cleats used to tow on the hip. The construction of both boats must unquestionably be strong enough to withstand the strains involved. A cleat that breaks or pulls off a deck can cause severe injuries.

• Rope Condition—The rope used for all of the towing lines must be strong enough for the job. Line that has been chafed, worn, or damaged must never be used. Dacron or other low-stretch rope is preferred.

• Hull Design—Not all boats can be lashed alongside one another without causing damage, no matter how many fenders are used. Be wary of large amounts of flare on a big boat that overhangs the cabin trunk or windshield of a smaller boat.

• Weather and Sea Conditions—Towing on the hip should only be done in calm water. Rough waves may cause the two boats to slam together despite all efforts at fendering. Anyone caught between the two hulls is certain to receive serious injuries.

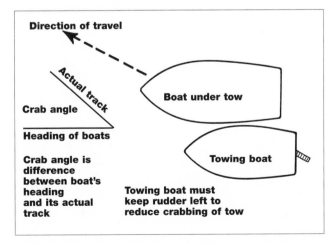

A tow makes crabwise headway when towing on the hip because of the off-center position of the towing boat's rudder and propeller.

One secret to towing on the hip is putting the stern of the towboat slightly *behind* the stern of the disabled craft. This position gives more maneuverability to the entire tow. Plenty of fenders are required to protect the two hulls from one another. Nylon rope should be avoided when towing on the hip because of its stretch. If possible, use Dacron or other low-stretch rope.

A minimum of three lines are used to bind the two boats together. Of the three, the towing strap does the majority of the work. This line leads from near the bow of the towing boat to the stern quarter of the disabled craft. The other two lines, the bow and stern breasts, hold the two boats tightly together. Additional breast or spring lines may be added as needed. All of these lines must be hauled tight so that the two boats move as one unit.

Speed when towing on the hip should be restricted to the minimum necessary for maneuverability. The two boats will not track in a straight line. Rather, they will "crab" toward the side opposite that on which the towing boat is secured. If the towboat is on the port side, the combined unit will crab left. Likewise, it will crab right if the towboat is on the port side. The unit will turn easily toward the direction of the crabbing, but will turn only reluctantly (if at all) in the opposite direction.

RIVER OR CANAL LOCKS

Locking through is the highlight of a canal or river cruise. It's also a time when skillful line handling is critical. Ropes are used to control the position of the boat in the lock as the water level goes up or down. Older locks require you to pay out or take in line to accommodate changing water levels. Locks serving large numbers of pleasure boats often have vertical steel cables to reduce onerous line handling. Newer locks on major commercial water-

Canada's Trent-Severn Waterway is just one of the scenic canal trips available in North America. Knowing how to handle lock lines is necessary for this type of cruising.

ways have floating bollards that eliminate the playing of long lock lines. Short docking lines are used to secure to the bollard, which goes up and down with the boat.

Locking upbound is always harder than downbound. Eddy currents caused by filling the lock on an upbound passage can be unexpectedly strong. They alternately pull the boat away from the lock wall and then slam it against rough concrete. Conversely, letting water out of the lock on a downbound trip creates few eddy currents. Your boat lies relatively quiet along the lock wall. Because of this difference, the number of crew needed to lock upbound is bigger than for a downbound passage. Two people may be enough to handle going down, but an upbound locking needs a crew of three or more on vessels over twenty-five feet in length.

All crew members need heavy work gloves to protect their hands when handling lines. Although it is not always required by law, everyone working on deck should wear a PFD. Eddy currents in a lock can make swimming difficult or impossible. Even skilled swimmers have drowned as the result of falling overboard in a lock.

The lockmaster is in charge of everything that goes on in his lock, including the use of ropes. An occasional lockmaster may have a unique personal requirement, but the general procedures have become standardized. Boats under twenty feet are often allowed to lock through using only a single line. Larger craft are always required to use two lines, one at the bow and the other at the stern. Most locks require shutting off all engines (including electric generators). Engine noise echoing off stone or concrete lock walls can overpower instructions from the lockmaster.

Long Ropes

Locking is hard, dirty work for the ropes involved. Not too many years ago it was standard for government locks to save money by purchasing less expensive manila rope for the

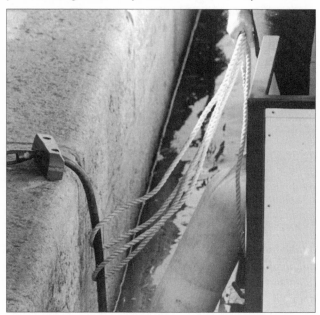

Locks primarily serving pleasure craft often have vertical steel cables to eliminate long lines. Looping a short dock line around a cable allows the boat to move up or down with the water level in the lock.

purpose. Today, manila is hard to find and may be equal in cost to low-price twisted-construction nylon rope. Dirty old nylon or polypropylene ropes are tossed down from the tops of lock walls. The rope may be synthetic, but the dirt and oil are as natural as ever.

Boat-Supplied Ropes

It is standard procedure for all vessels using locks to carry at least two working lines. Each of these ropes should be equal to *twice* the height (or *lift*) of the deepest lock plus at least 10 feet. For example, if the highest lock is 42 feet, then ropes should be at least 94 feet in length (42 x 2 = 84 + 10 = 94). Lock lines do not have to be quite as heavy as mooring ropes or anchor rodes. However, they should be at least $5/16$ inch in diameter for easy handling.

The requirement to carry lock lines does not mean that you will have to use them. Most locks provide lines or cables for pleasure boats to use. However, it's possible for the provided lines to become worn or damaged. In that case, boats locking through must depend upon their own lines.

When you enter the lock you will be directed to a specific place along one wall. Bow and stern lines are then passed to lock employees, who loop them around bollards so that both ends come back to the boat. Locking upbound requires heaving your lines to the top of the lock wall (a distance of perhaps 40 feet). One end of the doubled line may be secured to a cleat on your boat, but the other end *must* be kept free in the gloved hands of a crew member. Both ends are never secured to the boat because of the danger of becoming "hung up" on the lock wall. If the strain becomes too much for one person to hold, the working end of the line can be surged under the horn of a cleat.

Rope is let out or taken in as the water level changes in the lock. Once the gates open, it's a simple matter to let go of one end of the doubled

Don't Get Hung Up!

Lock lines should never be secured to both the boat and the top of the lock wall at the same time. To do so invites hanging the vessel on its lines if the water level in the lock goes down. Always be sure that one end of the line is free to be cast off immediately in an emergency.

line and pull on the other to haul it back aboard. Lines are normally handled from the side of the boat against the lock wall. Old-timers, however, often walk across the deck to the side of the boat *away* from the wall. This gives a larger angle, which affords greater control of the boat, especially in deeper locks.

Lock-Supplied Lines

Where the lock supplies the lines, the ropes are inevitably the scuzziest, dirtiest, and roughest cordage imaginable. Expect this filthy hunk of twisted fiber to come spiraling down without warning from an often unseen lock employee at the top of the wall. (Some lock employees seem to delight in catching pleasure boat crews unaware.) Gloves are a must for hand protection and *very* old clothes are suggested.

Never tie a lock-supplied rope to a deck cleat. The upper end will always be firmly secured to a bollard. If the boat end is cleated off, the possibility exists that the boat will become hung on its lines should the water level in the lock go down. Instead, surge the line under one horn of a cleat. This allows line to be taken in or paid out as necessary.

Vertical Wire Cable

Locks frequented by pleasure boats usually have vertical wire cables spaced at regular intervals along both walls. These cables eliminate the job of handling long lines. Instead, a short length of rope is looped loosely around the cable. This loop rides up or down the cable as the water level changes in the lock.

Many "river rats" (local slang for old hands at river cruising) make up special snap hook arrangements to use on vertical cables. The hooks are attached to short lengths of rope that are secured to the vessel about amidships. These hooks are snapped over the appropriate cables for the trip up or down in the lock. A quick

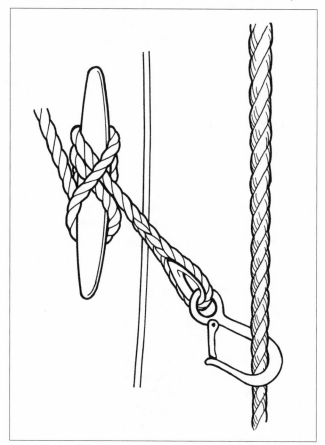

A snap hook makes using a vertical cable even easier. The pendant of this one is secured to the cleat partially hidden by the boat's railing. The hook rides up and down on the cable as the water level in the lock changes.

flick releases the hook when the gates open and the boat is free to continue on its way. A snap hook placed near the middle of its length is often sufficient to handle downbound trips for house-boats of sixty-five feet in length.

Snap hooks and loops of rope have both been known to become jammed on vertical cables. For this reason they should never be left unattended while the water level in the lock is changing.

Floating Bollards
Locks built in recent years by the U.S. Army Corps of Engineers are equipped with floating bollards. Secure to them in the same manner as you would to bollards on a regular wharf. Spring lines can be set to control fore-and-aft movement of the boat along the lock wall. Since these bollards are floating in the same water as the boat, their relationship to the vessel does not change as the water level goes up or down in the lock. Floating bollards do not require any adjustment of the lines while locking, nor are they likely to jam.

Fenders for Locking Through
Lock walls are notorious for being unfriendly to fiberglass gel coats. The importance of having adequate fenders *on both sides* of the boat cannot be overemphasized. Fenders are needed port and starboard because there is no predicting on which side of the lock you will be directed to tie up. You must quickly obey the instructions of the lockmaster. Switching fenders from one side to another becomes an irksome task on a major river or canal where it's not uncommon to pass through six or eight locks a day.

Fenders for use in locks are optimally a size or two larger than those for ordinary docking. Larger size accommodates rough treatment from being slammed into concrete lock walls by strong eddy currents. Also, fenders for locking need extra-strong attachment points and ropes because they come under considerable strain when dragged up a lock wall as the boat moves with the water level. Because of the strains involved, fenders should never be hung from lifelines or handrails when locking through. Instead, attach them to spring cleats or through-bolted metal toe rails capable of withstanding rough treatment.

INFLATED RUBBER OR VINYL FENDERS

These must be oversize to get the job done. Even so, the rough treatment leaves them looking old before their time. It may be possible to hang cylindrical fenders horizontally so they will "roll" up or down the lock wall. Do not use terry-cloth fender covers in a lock as they are sure to be shredded.

WOVEN ROPE (NATURAL-FIBER) FENDERS

These take the punishment from lock walls in stride, but are difficult to purchase. Also, natural-fiber fenders are subject to rot if put away wet.

FENDER BOARDS

These are hung horizontally across either inflated rubber or woven rope fenders. They absorb much of the rough treatment, but may be difficult to keep in position. Fender boards are also difficult to stow once the trip through the locks is complete.

HAY BAGS

Until recently, these were the traditional fenders for yachts transiting the Welland Canal, which bypasses Niagara Falls. Hay in burlap bags (later woven plastic canvas) provided an excellent cushioning effect. Such bags were popular because they were cheap but have fallen out of favor owing to the mess involved.

TIMBER BALKS

These can be hung vertically at intervals along the length of the hull. They should have a sloped top to minimize the chance of becoming caught on lock wall cracks. The bottoms hang six or eight inches above the boat's waterline. Let the wood absorb the punishment from the rough lock walls. Pad the side of the balk that lies against

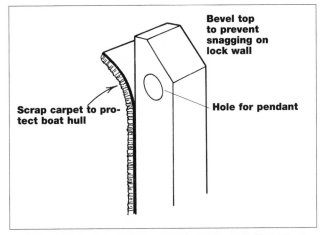

A timber balk fender can be made out of 4x4 stock. Bevel the top to prevent snagging on lock walls. Glue scrap carpet to the back to protect the hull. A hole through the timber allows attaching a pendant.

the boat with scrap carpet. Glue the carpet to the timber. Tack heads can scratch gel coat.

One type of homemade fender is illegal in almost all locks—old tires. Lockmasters hate old tires because they sometimes sink and become tangled in the sluice valve mechanism that controls water level in the lock. Removing an old tire can require several days of expensive repairs during which the lock is out of service to all traffic.

APPENDIX

ANCHOR DESCRIPTIONS

A wide variety of anchor styles and types are available. Many are produced and sold only in small geographic regions. The following list focuses on anchors produced by the major manufacturers (in parentheses) and sold throughout the United States.

Bruce Anchor—developed in Scotland to secure floating oil rigs. Sets quickly and reseats easily if the boat swings. Good holding in most bottoms except grass. This anchor's unusual shape makes it difficult to stow. (Mooring, Inc.)

Commando Small Craft Anchor System—developed for military raiding craft, this package contains an anchor, rope, chain, and shackle for boats up to sixteen feet. (Nav-X Corp.)

CQR Anchor—the original plow-style anchor. Made of drop-forged, high-tensile steel. Drop forging alters the grain structure of the steel, increasing its strength. Penetrates most bottoms, including weeds. Hooks coral and rocks. Limited holding power in mud. Heavy and difficult to stow. (Simpson Lawrence USA)

Danforth Deep-Set—a patented anchor designed to deliver high holding power. The thin, heat-treated shank flexes under load and springs back to its original shape after release. This helps the anchor stay dug into the bottom. Best in sand or mud; problems in coral, rock, or grass. (Rule Industries, Inc.)

Danforth Deep-Set Hi-Tensile—similar to above, but made of heat-treated chrome molybdenum steel. Somewhat expensive, but carries a limited lifetime warranty. (Rule Industries, Inc.)

Danforth Deep-Set VSB—a new design for very soft bottoms, this anchor is intended for use in muddy bottoms such as Chesapeake Bay. It has a shortened stock and extra-wide flukes. (Rule Industries, Inc.)

Danforth Hi-Tensile—high strength comes from the use of chrome molybdenum alloy steels. Hot-dipped galvanized for corrosion protection. Best in sand or mud; problems in grass, rock, or coral. (Rule Industries, Inc.)

Danforth Standard—the industry standard since the 1930s, it is made from high-strength steel. Good holding power at an economical price. Hot-dipped galvanized for corrosion protection. Best in sand; problems in coral, rock, or grass. (Rule Industries, Inc.)

Dor-More Pyramid—the special inverted pyramid shape of this permanent mooring anchor outholds mushroom and concrete block anchors. (Dor-Mor, Inc.)

Fortress Anchor—made of high-tech hardened aluminum-magnesium alloy. Disassembles for storage. Adjustable fluke angles for sand (32 degrees) or mud (45 degrees). A premium quality product, but expensive. Light weight allows anchor to "fly" in current. (Nav-X Corp.)

Guardian Utility Anchor—made from high-tensile, corrosion-resistant aluminum-magnesium alloy. Good performance at a competitive price, otherwise similar to Fortress anchor. (Nav-X Corp.)

Hans C-Anchor—This unique lightweight anchor is made of hot-dipped galvanized steel. Its two wishbone flukes pivot so the anchor always lands on the bottom ready to penetrate. Best in sand.

Problems in weed. (Hans C-Anchor, Inc.)

Harborfast Hi-Blade—incorporates the same plow design as the CQR in a lower-cost anchor. Performs well in most seabeds except mud. (Simpson Lawrence USA)

Manta Ray—a permanent anchor that is driven into the bottom, then rotated like a toggle bolt using a hydraulic tool. Anchor load and soil load-bearing capacity are accurately gauged. (Foresight Products, Inc.)

N.-S.R.-A.F. Self-Releasing—a navy-type anchor for anchoring in areas where stone, share, or sunken logs are likely to foul an anchor. Sliding ring on shank allows pulling this anchor out backward. Cast iron semisteel flukes, cold-rolled shank and ring. (Roloff Mfg. Corp.)

R.S.-V.C. River—a modern version of the traditional angler's mushroom anchor. For use in muck, sand, and weed. Will hold in stone and gravel. Available in vinyl-coated or aluminum finish. (Rolloff Mfg. Corp.)

Talon Anchor—an improved plow-style anchor designed to increase holding in mud and soft bottoms. Design includes special "mud wing" to improve penetration and a "mud hole" attachment point for rode. (Davis Anchors)

INDEX